Things Japanese

Things Japanese

Text by Nicholas Bornoff
Photos by Michael Freeman

PERIPLUS

Published by Periplus Editions (HK) Ltd,
with editorial offices at 130 Joo Seng Road,
#06-01, Singapore 368357

ISBN-13: 978-962-593-782-3
ISBN-10: 962-593-782-X

Printed in Singapore

Distributed by:
North America, Latin America & Europe
Tuttle Publishing, 364 Innovation Drive,
North Clarendon, VT 05759-9436, USA
Tel: (802) 773 8930; Fax: (802) 773 6993
Email: info@tuttlepublishing.com
www.tuttlepublishing.com

Asia Pacific
Berkeley Books Pte Ltd,
130 Joo Seng Road, #06-01/03,
Singapore 368357
Tel: (65) 6280 3320; Fax: (65) 6280 6290
Email: inquiries@periplus.com.sg
www.periplus.com

Japan
Tuttle Publishing, Yaekari Building, 3F
5-4-12 Osaki, Shingawa-ku
Tokyo 141-0032
Tel: (813) 5437 0171; Fax: (813) 5437 0755
Email: tuttle-sales@gol.com

10 09 08 07 06
8 7 6 5 4

Contents

Foreword

Outside Japan, the words 'things Japanese' often conjure concepts which the Japanese themselves would greet, at best, with indulgent smiles. *Netsuke*, *inrō*, iron kettles, swords and so on—all items that began to go out of fashion when Japan started to open its doors to the outside world following the Meiji restoration of 1868. You could add things like tea ceremony ceramics, paintings on sliding screen doors, tatami mats, stone lanterns and kimono to the list—even though these are alive and well. Some Japanese construe these attributes as grossly antiquated stereotypes, and are likely to resent it when foreigners acclaim them. "Kimono! Geisha! Fuji-yama", they fume, despite the fact that they all not only still exist, but are also exalted by many Japanese (who still wear kimono on special occasions) themselves. They may scoff at 'Fuji-yama' (the Japanese have never called their most famous mountain anything but 'Fuji-san') but, oh, how often one sees travel posters of Mt Fuji with girls in kimono—often holding paper umbrellas for good measure—deployed in the corridors of train stations!

The cutting edge of high technology is undeniably more the stuff of modern Japan than the samurai sword, but several venerable swordsmiths designated 'Living National Treasures' still forge the world's finest blades, just as they did centuries ago. Although obviously diminished, the proliferation of traditional arts and crafts in modern Japan is astonishing. With the introduction of the three-piece suit in the 1870s, *inrō* (the little tiered medicine boxes hanging from the kimono belt) may have gone the way of *netsuke* (the amazing miniature sculptures used to toggle them) but the skills of the craftsmen making them remain very much alive, albeit for different applications. Workshops in Kanazawa and Kyoto still make exquisite painted, embroidered or tie-dyed silk textiles; craftsmen all over Honshu and Kyushu continue to produce outstanding ceramics. Japanese lacquerware finds few rivals worldwide; many modern Japanese, whether serious calligraphers or just for writing seasonal greetings, keep a lacquer writing box complete with brushes and ink-stone. Notwithstanding the ferro-concrete urban sprawl, the wooden Japanese house still exists—in many cases just as an interior in a high rise apartment. Some people continue to paint traditional screen doors and, during the summer months especially, everyone likes to sprawl on the cool, comfortable smoothness of the tatami floor.

Many of those old Japanese objects have not lost their relevance, and continue to define the country producing them. People living outside Japan or those interested in its culture travel thousands of miles to the country not to see cars, computers and home entertainment equipment, but to visit the Japan that still uses those 'things Japanese'. Among the Japanese themselves, plenty would happily agree that many such objects remain signifiers of their culture, even if they have never seen them.

To foreigners, these things are the faint embers of a cultural love affair that started burning in the 19th century. It was fired first from woodblock prints, brought to the notice of Europe by France's Goncourt brothers and the impressionist painters. Then it burned all the more fiercely among those travelling to the hitherto hermit nation shortly after its doors first creaked open to the outside world. Believing that such exquisite items could only come from some kind of Fairyland, many of those early lovers of things Japanese were perhaps blinded and naïve. However warped their perceptions, the 'things Japanese' they so loved remain, and often flourish. Today, often sought by antique collectors, some are just the stuff of fond memorabilia, but many remain topical and are in everyday use.

House and Garden

Coming from homes designed to shut them off from the outside, Western visitors to Japan of a century or more ago were impressed. Light, airy and made of wood and paper, the traditional Japanese house merely enclosed the space outside, on to which it opened out. The furnishing was sparse, decoration minimal. From the veranda there was a landscape garden to contemplate, a pleasure more feasible now in the nearest park or temple precinct. Wooden houses and shops are becoming rare in modern Japan. Yet even in high-rise urban neighbourhoods, the past lives on often in the lacquerware and fine china the inhabitants reserve for special occasions, in the tatami matting, paper doors, screens and futon bedding. And out on the balconies, the gardens survive in the types of plants tended, and the proliferation of bonsai trees.

Shikki

漆器
lacquerware

Although they abhored cluttering their stark interiors, when the wealthy Japanese set out to impress visitors, they did it often with lacquerware. Writing boxes, trays and tableware, tea caddies and boxes for incense requisites or *bentō* (packed lunches), chests for travelling or storing special clothes (see right): all of these were exquisitely decorated by master artisans. Black, red, yellow or multicoloured, the gleaming lacquer often enhanced elaborate designs made from powdered gold and silver (*maki-e*) or inclusions of metal and mother-of-pearl. Japan knows a thing or two about lacquer, as Europeans were aware long before it opened its doors to the outside world; during the 18th century, English furniture makers simply called the process 'japanning'.

The Japanese call items so treated *nuri-mono* (coated things), but the term referring more specifically to the craft itself is *shikki*, which translates more closely. It had long been assumed that the technique made its way into Japan via the ancient Sino-Korean connection; there are fine examples of 1,300-year-old lacquerware in the temple treasure houses of Nara. But archaeological sites in Japan have recently yielded lacquered wooden fragments; carbon dating puts them in the middle of the neolithic Jōmon period (10,000–300BC).

Called *urushi* in Japanese and used in most of East Asia, the substance itself comes from the sap of a tree (*Rhus vernicifera*). Tapped like latex, it is filtered and heated before being used to coat various materials, especially wood or leather. Unlike other varnishes, it requires no solvent. Resistant to heat, water and natural corrosives, its hardness is such that it was used to coat the leather breast-plates on samurai suits of armour.

Shikki production is typically a community venture. In Narai, in Nagano prefecture's Kiso Valley, local artisans work in teams as they have done for 300 years. Some deal with woodwork, including bowls, trays, boxes and furniture. Bowls are coated with red or black lacquer by artisans seated on the floor of a workshop occupied by their forebears for generations. After several coats, the objects may go on to be decorated by painters before being lacquered again. Following each application, they are turned overnight in a clockwork drying cabinet. The lacquered products must always remain in a humid environment; perhaps high precipitation and humid summers partly explain why Japanese lacquerware is quite as good as it is.

The Japanese brought a peerless degree of refinement to lacquerware. There are centres all over Japan, including several among the sub-tropical Okinawan islands famous for their bold, colourful designs. Out of several claimants for being the first producers, Fukui prefecture's Echizen-shikki is said to have originated during the 6th century. Going back to the Heian period (792–1185), Kyoto's Kyō-shikki is one of the most beautiful, and many fine pieces were made for the tea ceremony between the 14th and 16th centuries. Like many Japanese crafts, *shikki* is regarded as having reached its apogee during the 18th century. It was then that the technique known as *maki-e* was at its most exquisite and extravagant.

With many craftsmen following in the footsteps of their forebears, *shikki* is alive and well and the range greater than ever. Fabulously expensive lacquered chests are still being wrought by renowned traditional masters, alongside innovative items in bold modern designs. And the soup accompanying any Japanese meal will always be served in a lacquered bowl. You see them piled high on the shelves of local supermarkets in red and black and patterned with gold. Cheap, cheerful and, more often than not, made of plastic.

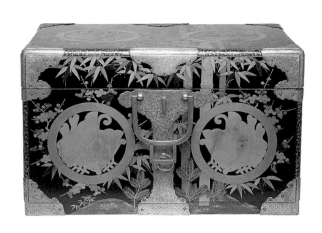

Tansu

簞笥
wooden chests

Some Japanese insist that having four seasons makes Japan unique. Japan has *haru*, *natsu*, *aki* and *fuyu* (spring, summer, autumn and winter) and that makes it quite different from anywhere else. This could be construed as obdurate patriotic myopia, but what may well be at work here is a curious historical precedent. Everyone changes their wardrobe according to the season, but no one made more of a fanfare of it than did the Japanese during the Edo period (1603–1868). Ever mindful of keeping up appearances, people would practically turn the seasonal change of wardrobe into a pageant. Apart from clothes, this revolved also around an item of furniture containing them, a wooden chest called a *tansu*.

Tansu were mainly kept in the *kura*, a storehouse with massive, fire-proof clay walls which stood either next to the house itself or sometimes a little further up the street. The *tansu* with winter clothes were brought back in spring and the *tansu* that contained spring wear replaced them. In the wealthier households, the boxes were borne back and forth by liveried servants. Most typically, a *tansu* consists of upper and lower halves, each containing two drawers. Many are fronted with cupboard doors. The upper and lower sections have metal handles at both ends, which are in fact loops for passing a shoulder-pole.

Contrived to impress neighbours and passers-by, *tansu* often displayed outstanding carpentry and craftsmanship, sometimes with wonderfully decorative open-work iron fittings and lacquered finishes, but they were not designed to be admired at home. Except for tables for eating and writing upon, rooms in traditional Japanese homes are kept pointedly uncluttered with furniture. Instead they have built-in closets with sliding doors which, until Western influences took hold in the 1870s, were used for hiding away the *tansu*.

There were in fact several different kinds of *tansu*; they were neither solely for clothes nor for storing in a closet or *kura*. Several varieties were destined solely for the kitchen; more or less permanent fixtures and often fitted with cupboard doors above and drawers below, they are known sometimes as *mizuya* and were mainly used for keeping utensils and tableware. There were ship-board *tansu*, travelling *tansu* and *tansu* designed for use in shops; there were *tansu* that were strong-boxes. There was even one kind of fairly heavy kitchen *tansu* with wooden wheels—unlike the Western chest-of-drawers, the *tansu* was always made with easy removal and transportation in mind.

One of the more curious variants is the *kaidan* (staircase) *tansu* (see left). Though technically free-standing, they were designed to be incorporated into the house and, as such, constituted the staircase. Many old houses have been demolished in recent decades, along with their *kaidan tansu*, but fortunately, now that antique furniture fever has belatedly gripped Japan, such salvageable items are now borne away and sold.

Tansu have always been made in many places in Japan, but among the finest antique varieties are those from Yonezawa in North-eastern Honshu, renowned for expensive *keyaki* (zelkova) wood. Other woods used for *tansu* are *sugi* (Japanese cedar), *hinoki* (Japanese cypress) and, above all, lightweight, pale *kiri* (pawlonia) wood.

Today, the Japanese have also widely taken to having *tansu* in their homes—especially the growing legions of people fond of antiques. Like Korean chests, fine *tansu* fetch high prices on the international antique market. Reproductions are now common and, though still cheap 20 years ago, even modest examples of the genuine article have become relatively expensive.

Noren

暖簾

entrance curtains

Originally contrived as a sunshade, the *noren* curtain is among the most traditional of things Japanese, and one that never seems to go out of fashion. Like so many things, it is often said to have originated in China, making its way long ago into Japan with the devotional paraphernalia associated with Buddhism. The merchants attending temple services must have taken note; during the Kamakura period (1185–1333), the *noren* came to be used as a sign to hang over the entrances to shops. Made of thick cotton or hemp, the most basic form of *noren* shows characters or a white logo applied in the centre with a resist-dyeing technique on a dark indigo background, though colours and designs nowadays tend to vary a great deal.

The logo almost always represents the specialty of the house. A pattern suggesting a tea whisk and/or tea bowl, for instance, would denote a shop selling tea. The phonetic Japanese character *yu*—meaning hot water— is found on the *noren* hanging outside the entrance of the traditional public bath. *Noren* are commonly decorated with the owner's *mon*, or family crest. White on a dark background, these ingeniously simple patterns represent birds (typically a crane) or animals, a tree or plant (pawlonia, ginko leaves), a

mountain (especially Mt Fuji), a flower (the imperial *mon* is the chrysanthemum) or a Chinese character. In addition to *noren*, they adorn clothing such as workmen's jackets (*hanten*) (see pages 52–53) or kimono (see pages 54–55), stationery (see pages 74–77) and lanterns (see pages 120–121).

Traditional restaurants, *sembei* biscuit makers and craft shops alike display the *mon* of the founder or owner. Boasting a history of several generations, some businesses earn a great deal of prestige. In much the same way as the master of any art or craft, a chef or confectioner may take on pupils, and when one of them is ready to open their own shop, the master may grant them the use of the house name. After all, for centuries Japanese craftsmen have customarily adopted their master's name. Although not necessarily dependent on its predecessor, the new shop is permitted to use the same logo and *noren* as the parent institution. This is considered a great honour. The operative expression is *noren wo wakeru* (to divide the *noren*), implying membership of a family.

Threaded over a bamboo pole by means of loops, the *noren* is suspended over the shop entranceway. Depending on the width, it may be divided up into two, three or four

panels (though occasionally more) and it generally reaches down to cover only about a quarter of the entrance—all this being devised to make it easier for the customer to enter. If you see a *noren* over the entrance, it means the shop is open. Having rolled the *noren* up around the pole at closing time, the staff take it away altogether before they lock up and go home. Longer *noren* leave only the bottom quarter of the entranceway uncovered. This kind will usually only be split into two panels. They often front cheap drinking haunts known as *ippai nomiya*, though traditionally these have a curtain made of hanging lengths of straw rope called *nawa noren*. These days *nawa noren* is a common expression denoting any cheap drinking dive—whether it actually has one fronting the entrance or not.

Long sought for providing cool shade in summer, *noren* are also a common fixture in private homes. Although they often deploy contemporary designs of a high standard, including abstract calligraphy and subtle modernist renditions of traditional designs and colours, decorative *noren* these days can depict anything. This includes western floral motifs, garish copies of Utamaro woodblock prints, kittens, puppies, Japanese children's cartoon characters and—yes—Mickey Mouse.

Yoshizu

葭簀
marsh-reed screens

Most people associate *yoshizu* with summer. This comes first in the television commercials, almost as soon as the last cherry blossoms have dropped from the trees, when it is still spring. Nubile beauties in teeny swimsuits luxuriate in the turquoise Okinawan shallows; bright blue arrows of coolness blast from sleek air conditioners over idealized interiors. The commercials warn too of summer setbacks. It's hot and humid; the Japanese, like the British, open conversations with remarks about the weather. In summer, *"Atsui desu ne*?" ("Isn't it hot?") is heard around the clock.

The commercials also warn of the approach of bug season, vividly depicting armies of *gokiburi* (cockroaches) and mosquitoes being effectively exterminated by chemical means. Though no less glued to TV commercials, people in the countryside often still prefer *katori senkō* or mosquito-removing incense. Green and shaped into a spiral, this sends pungent—though not unpleasant—smoke drifting up under the roofs of older houses.

Katori senkō is burned mainly by traditionalists, the kind of people who also put up *yoshizu* (marsh-reed screens) against their windows and open doors to provide shade from the harsh summer sun. Traditional restaurants generally put up *yoshizu* too,

notably specialists in soba noodles—a year-round Japanese staple popularly eaten cold in a variety of ways in summer. *Sōmen*, white noodles so thin and translucid that they look ethereal, are often served in bowls floating with ice cubes. They're not exactly substantial, which is just as well, as Japan's sweltering canicular season is very debilitating and causes a loss of appetite. The term *natsuyase* (summer thinness) has been used to identify the effect for centuries.

Some believe the antidote lies in eating eels. Folk legend has it that the custom was initiated by a wily 18th-century scholar, who was really in cahoots with the eel merchants. Behind the *yoshizu* of today's traditional eel restaurants, plenty of people still seek this high-protein fish as a summer treat. Meanwhile, *yoshizu* go up too to provide shade as well as partitioning in beer gardens. Situated often on the roofs of department stores, one finds adepts here quaffing tankards of chilled brew from tumbler to bucket size.

Yoshizu are erected in front of traditional dessert shops too, where kids eat shaved ice topped with syrups coming in an amazing array of garish colours. There are inumerable fairs and festivals all around Japan in summer; one to look out for is Obon, the Buddhist

festival of the dead. Obon is the time for
lantern festivals, when families pay respect to
deceased relatives and light fireworks outside
their homes. In downtown Tokyo in Ueno,
summer finds families dressed in *yukata* (see
page 55) strolling through evening plant
markets, the stalls being partitioned with
(what else?) *yoshizu*. Along here too they sell
insects. The lovely firefly, now vanished from
polluted cities, blinks brightly in little bamboo
cages along with the *suzumushi* (bell crickets)
whose enchanting, high-pitched ringing
sound can turn even the most sultry night
idyllically cool. You find too the kind of insects
children stalk with butterfly nets in the day-
time, especially rhino beetles and, later in the
season, *semi* (Japanese crickets).

The shrill whirring of the *semi* in fact
heralds summer's end—stifling as it still is in
late August. Everyone moans about the heat
but once the insect orchestra falls silent and
it's all over, most people are looking forward
to saying *"atsui desu ne?"* again next year.
And bringing out the *yoshizu*.

Byōbu

屏風
painted screens

No one knows when *byōbu* first appeared, but 8th-century Japanese historical records report that they had been presented to the emperor by a Korean ambassador in 686. Like most continental novelties, *byōbu* were at first used exclusively by the aristocracy. In pre-medieval times, the aristocratic dwelling was large, single-storied and, as now in the Japanese house, featured sliding panels to divide the rooms. The Japanese predilection for screens was a result of the hot, humid summer weather; sliding panels allowed air to circulate, but also provided shelter from drafts (*byōbu* translates as 'wind shelter'). They also provided privacy if needed.

Minimalism has always been of the essence in Japanese art, but if the walls of a dwelling were to remain pristine, one could instead decorate panels and partitions, thus several different kinds of screen developed. One was the *byōbu*; they served as canvasses in a kind of painting called *shōheki-ga*.

Mainly religious, but in some cases secular as well, early Japanese art had always been executed in the Chinese style. Then because of the increasing popularity of *emaki* (picture scrolls) during the Heian period, narrative, historical and naturalist themes developed relatively free of outside influences. This style

was known as *Yamato-e* (Japanese pictures), and the Chinese style came to be known as *kara-e* (outside pictures). Both were used on *byōbu*, but in the relatively austere Kamakura era (1185–1333), *byōbu* were mainly decorated with Chinese-style ink paintings.

During the strife-torn Muromachi period (1333–1568), lavishly painted and gilded *byōbu* became fashionable among shoguns eager for ostentatious trimmings in their new villas and castles. The master of the Kanō school, notably Motonobu (1476–1559) and Eitoku (1543–1590), brought *shōheki-ga* to its zenith, blending elements of *kara-e* and *Yamato-e* together. Consisting usually of two, three, four, or six panels, *byōbu* often came in pairs; a landscape or scene with figures ran continuously from one screen to the next.

Byōbu became more common during the Edo period (1603–1868), when the Rimpa school founded by Sōtatsu and exemplified by Ogata Kōrin (1658–1716) came to the fore. It emphasized decorative composition, further developed in the 18th century by Itō Jackuchō with his remarkable animal and bird designs. In the 19th century, *shōheki-ga* generally became formulaic, mainly comprising pallid emulations of late medieval masterpieces. Painters working on *byōbu* today are scarce.

Shōji

障子
sliding paper screens

One of the most defining things about the Japanese traditional home is the *shōji*. Either a paper sliding door or a sliding paper screen, it shouldn't be confused with the *fusuma*—a sliding paper door of a different kind. Covered with thick paper, the *fusuma* are opaque and their function is as room dividers or cupboard doors. Often magnificently adorned by master painters in the past, today they are still often quite prettily decorated.

The *shōji* on the other hand are absolutely plain. Consisting of panels of latticed wood covered on one side with thin white paper, the *shōji* slide in grooves and are placed immediately behind the windows of a house. A traditional Japanese room thus requires no curtains. Fitted with solid wooden panels at the bottom, *shōji* are also used as doors to rooms facing a corridor with windows; many traditional Japanese houses have a corridor running around the front and sides of the house both upstairs and down. The *shōji* date back to a time when there were no window panes, so having the rooms set back from the windows via a corridor ensured one could stay dry in all but the most severe weather.

In fact, until glass came to be adopted increasingly from the end of the 19th century, the *shōji* were what would be described in the west as windows. The Japanese word *mado* (window) really refers only to the window cavity. The *shōji* were placed inside or just behind it; the windows along the corridor would thus be fitted with *shōji* just like the doors facing them. To prevent getting the outer *shōji* wet if it rained hard, one had to slide the *amado*, a solid wooden shutter, closed in front of the window. The pre-modern Japanese must have spent a lot of their rainy days in semi-darkness.

In fairer weather, the *shōji* imbue a room with a lovely diffuse light as white as that reflected from snow. Even after window glass had become widely adopted, frosted glass was often used in the outer *shōji* to achieve the same effect. Window glass in traditional Japanese houses is otherwise perfectly transparent, the window frames frequently being shaped exactly like the *shōji* of old.

Tending to yellow fairly quickly, the paper used in these screens ideally needs replacing about once a year. *Shōji* are also notoriously fragile and are forever being torn—especially in households with small people with busy little fingers. If one can't be bothered to replace the entire panel, the alternative is to stick a little square of *shōji* paper over the hole. About a century ago the repair was a little more elaborate; people would often cut out the replacement piece in a variety of shapes—often birds or animals for the amusement of the perpetrators of the mishap.

Travelling around Japan in 1905, British photographer Herbert Ponting aroused great curiosity in children in country inns. "Not only do Japanese rooms have ears," he commented about the flimsy walls, "but they have eyes as well. It is quite a common occurrence to see a human one peeping through some small hole in the *shōji*. Occasionally you may detect a finger in the act of making such a hole or enlarging one already made." And once, in the dead of night, he threw open the *shōji* "in time to see three pairs of heels flying down the corridor… while shouts of laughter filled the narrow passage from the inquisitive *nē-sans* (girls) who owned them."

Ukiyo-e

浮世絵
woodblock prints

Holding pride of place out of all things Japanese in western eyes, *ukiyo-e* were one of the items which no serious 19th-century travellers to Japan failed to bring back home with them. *Ukiyo-e* began not as woodblock prints as such, but as a style of painting in the mid 17th century. Melding the styles of the Tosa school (purely Japanese genre painting) and the Kano school (Japanese reworking of Chinese painting) together, the exponents sought subject matter for their *e* (pictures) in the *ukiyo* (the floating world)—the term coined for the urban pleasure quarters grudgingly conceded by the dictatorial Tokugawa shoguns, the rulers of Japan between 1603 and 1867.

Combining all the provinces of pleasure of Edo (Tokyo) together—Kabuki theatre, tea-houses, taverns, restaurants and brothels —'the floating world' was the haunt of high fashionistas and constituted a crucible for Japanese culture. Focusing on subjects like geisha, prostitutes, Kabuki actors, erotica and aspects of contemporary life, *ukiyo-e* also embraced historical subjects, landscapes, ghost stories, naturalism and still-life. Lasting some 150 years, and still highly collectible today, the genre still presents us with a window on a vanished world.

The popularization of *ukiyo-e* is generally attributed to Hishikawa Moronobu (1618–94), a prominent book illustrator who pioneered the single print. Many of the books of the day (for example, *warai-bon*; laughing books) were designed for the titillation of the townsman; much of the output was graphically erotic *shunga* (spring pictures). The skills *ukiyo-e* artists displayed with using colour and texture to depict clothing found many prints dubbed 'brocade pictures'; these artists were nothing if not versatile. Dabhands at pornography, Harunobu (1724–70) and his contemporary Koryūsai also made many charming prints of pleasure quarter girls doing more mundane things; the same applied even more to the great Utamaro (1750–1806) whose celebrated *bijin-ga* (beautiful person pictures) are masterpieces both of composition and technical skill. Capable of consummate depictions of anything and everything (including sex), the innovative Katsuhika Hokusai (1760–1849) also widened the horizons of the medium with many landscapes and travel themes, a genre greatly popularized by Andō Hiroshige (1797–1858).

Although some *ukiyo-e* had reached Europe earlier in the 19th century via the Dutch (the only people other than Chinese permitted to trade in Japan during the Edo period), it was in France that they had the most significant impact. Popular wisdom had it that the prints were used in Japan to wrap fish, and that they first came to the attention of French aesthetes because they were used to pack Japanese export chinaware. But the first of these notions is sheer nonsense, the second at best apocryphal. Opened in 1862 and renowned among connoisseurs of oriental art, a shop and tea salon called 'La Porte Chinoise' made its reputation above all from importing Japanese prints. The prints soon had a profound influence on French art, first of all on Manet and Degas, then on Toulouse-Lautrec, Monet, Van Gogh and the impressionists. Announcing bold new steps in design and asymmetrical composition, *ukiyo-e* changed the entire course of Western art and design.

The prints that were most popular abroad in the 1890s were already old as the great masters such as Utamaro and Hokusai had belonged to the century before. Produced in ever larger numbers and pandering increasingly to popular taste, *ukiyo-e* went into decline quite early in the 19th century. That said, there were still plenty of quality works around

伊豫守源義經

越中前司盛俊

produced by 'decadents' such as Toyokuni and Kunisada. Although *ukiyo-e* declined as such with the demise of the eponymous pleasure quarters, the woodblock print remained a medium of choice for many significant Japanese artists well into the modern era.

Tatami

畳
tatami mats

Despite the westernization of architecture in Japan during the past century, postwar reconstruction and later building sprees, some things never change. For all its ferro-concrete and glass and for all the wall-to-wall carpeting, even the highest modern residential apartment block may not be as thoroughly western as it first seems: living spaces within will usually contain at least one Japanese-style room—distinguished by tatami mats.

"Upon these mats the people eat, sleep, and die," wrote the American Japan-scholar Edward Morse in the 1880s, "they represent the bed, chair, lounge and sometimes table, combined." Though many families nowadays prefer a kitchen table, they will always dine around a low table on the tatami mats when there are guests. Western beds are becoming common, but many people still roll out futon bedding (see overleaf) straight onto the floor.

Tatami mats are also resilient, which is why foreigners often find sleeping on a comparatively thin futon far more comfortable than they anticipated.

Popular among the aristocracy during the 8th century, tatami mats were originally used as beds. In a world without chairs, the thin matting hitherto partially covering floors did little to alleviate the discomfort of hard wood, so tatami gradually came to be used as flooring too. Rules came about governing the size—the thickest being an Imperial preserve—but from the Edo period (1603–1868), tatami came to be used increasingly in ordinary homes.

Tatami mats each consist of thousands of stems of a rush called *igusa* tightly stitched together. Covered with very close-woven matting, tatami feel smooth to the touch. The sides are trimmed with thin decorative strips of fabric—the quality varying according to the price. Filling the house with a scent like new-mown hay, tatami are a light greyish-green when new, fading to warm yellow as they age. About 10 cm (4 in) thick, tatami are disposed according to set patterns; with eight mats and more, they describe a spiral around the central pair. Tatami mats absorb moisture, providing welcome coolness during the muggy, hot summers; another remarkable property is the recently discovered capacity for absorbing air pollutants such as exhaust gas.

The size of a Japanese room is expressed in terms of the number of tatami mats, running from two, three to four and a half, then six, eight, ten mats and upwards, following the twice-times table. The *yojōhan* (four-and-a-half mat room) is an exception devised because the Japanese shun the number four on its own. The number four is considered unlucky as the character to describe it can be pronounced 'shi', a homonym for the Japanese word for death.

Tatami sizes are standardized, but there are regional variants, *Kyō-ma* (from Kyoto) being slightly larger than the smallest *Kantō-ma* (Tokyo), with *Chūkyō-ma* (Nagoya) in between. When real estate offices advertise properties they often refer to the Kantō mat, 176 cm x 88 cm (5 ft 9 in x 3 ft), which is now pretty well the national standard—a sign of the current premium on space.

Until very recently there used to be a tatami maker in every neighbourhood but, in the wake of so many cheaper imports from Taiwan and China, their number is decreasing, but not dying out. The mats are generally imported bundled and stitched, but the cutting, covering and custom trimmings are mainly undertaken in Japan—where this beautiful and remarkably practical flooring concept is likely to remain in vogue for quite some time.

Futon

布団
futons

I was forewarned that I would be sleeping on a mattress on the floor when I first went to Japan in 1979, but it didn't bother me over much. The night I first entered my apartment, however, I was a little shaken. There was a bright red plastic television and pristine tatami matting, but nothing else at all—let alone a mattress. Sliding back the paper doors from the cupboard, to my relief, my friends took out a rolled-up mattress and quilt, and promptly made up the bed on the floor. This is the futon, loosely used to refer to bedding as a whole, but actually referring only to the mattress. Though the latter was only 12 cm (5 in) thick, it was cushioned by the resilience of the tatami matting and the arrangement was comfortable.

The futon had by then been through centuries of evolution in Japan. My futon was not, in fact, much like the original thing at all. Cotton on the outside, it was stuffed with a mixture of both natural and synthetic fibers —a combination that made it lighter and warmer than its all-cotton parent. The quilt was essentially a Western duvet. That said, the main ingredient of nearly all today's better futons is still cotton down—as it had been almost exclusively until after World War II, when there was a sharp increase in Western concepts and materials. For a while, until they

became standard, my kind of mattress was briefly called *yōfuton* (Western futon).

Even now, in some traditional inns you can find thin yet fairly heavy cotton futon— much as they were between the late 19th and early 20th centuries. They are only slightly better than sleeping right on the floor, which is why people often use two. In the Yoshiwara red-light district in the 1890s, the better class of demi-mondaines liked to boast about using several. To prove it, they would have the maids ostentatiously air them on the brothel balconies alongside quilts made of silks and satins. Today, bedding is still regularly festooned from Japan's more mundane window-ledges and balconies; humidity causes down to be compressed and lose its fluffiness, so futon need to be aired about once a week.

The futon originated in the 17th century, when the wealthy began using mattresses stuffed with cotton down. Everyone else had to make do with bags stuffed with flax, hemp, straw or rushes. In some fishing villages they stuffed their bedding with seaweed. Until quite recently, thickly padded and capacious garments with sleeves were worn in winter instead of quilts or coverlets. These days, over a third of futon in Japan and almost half the quilts are imported—both mainly from China.

Irori

囲炉裏
iron hearths

I remember a country-style tavern in a western suburb of Tokyo. Being directly beneath the elevated train tracks, it was none too bucolic, but although the trains rumbled intermittently overhead, it was hard to tell that you weren't in alpine Nagano prefecture. Wearing a rustic kimono of indigo cotton, Mama-san sat surrounded by a low, square counter of dark polished wood, pouring sake and taking orders as her husband toiled in the kitchen behind her. A long pot-hook hanging from a beam beneath the ceiling supported a large white metal tea-kettle. It was being heated over an *irori* fireplace—a square-shaped hearth just next to her. Close at hand she kept an oblong box of stainless steel, with four holes devised for heating flasks of sake. The box is actually a tank, filled with water kept constantly heated by the fire just next to it. It was very similar to the one in an illustration of an *irori* in Edward Morse's *Japanese Homes and their Surroundings* and captioned "The Best Fireplace". That is apparently how they rated the *irori* back in 1885; those contemplating the few still extant today would concur.

But in the rustic tavern in suburban Tokyo there was no fire, nor even embers. The sake-warming box was electric. All was artifice. It was just another of those countless city *furusato* (home-sweet-home) restaurants evoking a lost, idyllic rural past usually fondly imagined rather than actually remembered by the countless legions of urbanites of rural descent. This wasn't a real *irori* at all—the pot hook hung over a gas ring.

Real *irori* are still to be found above all in old houses in towns and villages in mountainous districts, and in farmhouses in particular. Houses like this often have very high roofs. There is no chimney, the smoke goes straight up and out in a hole at the top. The floor is raised like a platform and the *irori*, always square, is sunken into the planking. The base of the hearth is sand, mixed with fine ash, so that it is a uniform grey colour. The fire is concentrated in the centre. Made of wood or iron, the pot-hooks come in several different configurations, often dangling from a chain, which may also be fitted with a rack for smoking fish. Although places still having one today invariably also have a kitchen, they will still cook certain dishes over the *irori*—especially *nabemono* (pot stews).

In winter, the *irori* is as cheering to the Japanese as the pub fireplace is to the British. The first time I saw a genuine *irori* was at a

homely *minshuku* (family-owned inn) in Takayama; the couple running it insisted that guests should sit around it after dinner. There's no denying the *irori*'s congeniality; conversation lasted into the wee hours and the hangover in the morning was dire!

On the verge of total extinction 20 years ago, the *irori* has been making something of a comeback thanks to a heightened awareness of the importance of preserving the past in Japan. They are no longer much of a rarity in traditional style inns and restaurants; and among Japanese who are able to afford a second home in the countryside, the *irori* is the height of chic.

Hibachi

火鉢

portable charcoal braziers

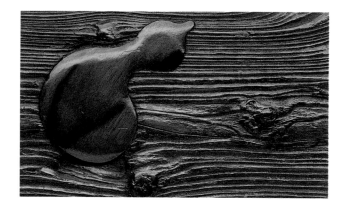

When you visit Japan's historic buildings, in many cases what you are seeing is either a replica of or a construction much later than the original, which transpires to have burned down during its long history—even several times. To be sure, the cause lay often in war and natural disaster or, occasionally, arson too. Whichever, these buildings were made of wood. The flames spread frequently from one to the next, which was often less than one metre (3 ft) away. In former times fires regularly burned down entire Japanese cities. When a blaze started in a home, it originated frequently in the kitchen or in careless use of the *ro*—a small sunken fireplace found often in the rooms of inns. The *ro* was used mainly for heating bedclothes, which were draped over a wooden frame above it, but accidents occurred when the fabric touched the embers.

Though only nominally safer, a much more popular and widespread alternative was the *hibachi*, a portable charcoal brazier. "Around the *hibachi*," observed one foreign visitor in 1907, "circulates not only the domestic but also the social life of Japan. All warm themselves at it; tea is brewed by means of it; guests are entertained, chess played, politics discussed beside it; secrets are told across it, and love made over it."

Of Chinese origin, *hibachi* were in use in Japan for well over a millennium. Round ones were often made of iron or bronze with handles, or ceramic (typically of thick, blue and white patterned porcelain) or cut into the bole of a tree. The section of trunk could be turned and smoothed to show the grain, then polished and perhaps carved with a decorative design or lacquered. Smoothed and polished, gnarled and irregularly shaped boles were popular too. Wooden *hibachi* were always fitted with a metal lining, usually of copper. Made of wood, the square or oblong *hibachi* incorporated a copper lining flush with the sides; sometimes it was just an open box into which a round *hibachi* was placed. The finest hibachi were often cabinets around 70 cm (2 ft 4 in) across and incorporating drawers for smoking requisites.

To prepare a *hibachi*, the fine ash within had to be raked up into a regular cone, the pieces of burning charcoal (brought from the kitchen or from a pan heated outdoors) were placed in the top. A sizeable piece of charcoal could burn for many hours. Although it was smokeless, the possibility of toxic fumes prompted people to carry the *hibachi* from the bedroom before retiring. The rake and tongs for handling charcoal were kept in the

hibachi along with such items as an iron stand for a kettle; a grid was often placed over the stand to grill food. It was customary to place a *hibachi*—however simple—before each guest, along with a rectangular wooden *tabako-bon* (tobacco box) (see pages 72–73) which contained a miniature *hibachi* and a cylindrical wooden spittoon.

Capable of warming a room adequately, the *hibachi* was a vital household item and often an heirloom. Old *hibachi* have had antiquarian value for a very long time in Japan where, although no longer used, they still do today. When in use they were greatly cherished. Edward Morse noticed that one would often observe a Japanese person absent-mindedly gazing into the embers and something more: "A sentiment prompts many families to keep the *hibachi* burning continually; I was told that in one family in Tokyo the fire had been kept alive continuously for over two hundred years."

Satsuma-yaki

薩摩焼
satsuma ware

The Shogun Toyotomi Hideyoshi's two attempts to invade Korea in 1592 and 1598 were dismal failures. But, taken with ceramics they discovered along the campaign trail, some of his generals came up with a brilliant idea for turning adversity into an asset. Rather than burden themselves with crates full of plundered pottery, they kidnapped the potters. Being regional governors, they saw ceramic production as a means of filling the provincial coffers. Although they were virtual prisoners, the Koreans nonetheless enjoyed a fairly exalted position in Kyushu. Small wonder. They were instrumental in inventing and propagating pottery techniques which made the ware from the Kyushu towns of Arita and Imari world famous in the next century.

Shimazu Yoshihisa, another of Hideyoshi's generals and lord of the Kyushu province of Satsuma (now Kagoshima), brought Korean potters back to his fiefdom too. Displaying the delicacy of porcelain, their particular specialty was a cream-coloured glaze covered with minute crackling. Despite its early popularity, the ware fell out of fashion and the Satsuma potteries declined. By the mid 19th century 'Old Satsuma' ware had become very rare and was much sought by collectors. Today there are precious few pieces outside of museums.

A different animal altogether, the newer form of Satsuma seen on these pages proved immensely popular in Europe. It was born of provincial governor Shimazu Shigehide's efforts to revive the flagging local pottery industry at the beginning of the 19th century, when he dispatched his potters around various centres in Japan in search of new techniques. They returned with the techniques of polychrome painting, learned in Kyoto's Kinkōzan pottery.

In 1827 Shigehide sent another potter to Kyoto to learn *kinran*—a 17th century method for applying gold to enhance red and white patterns—imitating polychrome *kinran* textile designs of Chinese origin adopted in Japan for centuries. Adapting what he learned to what he already knew, he and the other Satsuma potters produced a lavishly ornate hybrid. Although called Satsuma ware, it was produced only in Kyoto for some time. The finest craftsmen of the genre was a Kyotoite, Nin'ami Dōhachi, who specialized in white Satsuma decorated in the *nishiki* style which, like *kinran*, was inspired from textiles. Nin'ami opened the first exclusive Satsuma pottery in his own city—far indeed from the real Satsuma.

Hoping to take control of what they deemed should have been produced in their own kilns, the Satsuma governors sent another potter to Kyoto, who came back to launch the Naeshirogawa style which, comprising more colours, was (if such a thing were possible) even more ornate. Considered by many as the definitive Satsuma style, the ware not only faced competition from namesakes in Kyoto, but also spawned a rash of cheap imitators in pottery centres all over the country. Requiring minute precision, detailed designing and painterly skills, Satsuma ware is the product of extraordinary skill. Made almost exclusively for export, it appealed to the baroque and bombastic tastes of European courts. The work and paintings can be really exquisite, but in many cases the beauty of the objects is demeaned by sheer decorative over-kill. Praise was lavished on Satsuma ware at the Exposition Universelle in Paris in 1867; it perfectly fitted the times. Good pieces fetch high prices today, though most look as though they were designed solely for the ponderous and ostentatious Victorian drawing-room.

Imari-yaki

伊万里焼
imari ware

Strangely, with all the influence that China had had upon Japan, the Japanese adopted porcelain over a millennium after the Chinese had invented it. Japanese ceramics had long consisted almost entirely of stoneware. In the late 15th century, Chinese porcelain was being increasingly imported, fuelling the growth of the aristocratic craze for the tea ceremony. Tea ceremony or not, the vogue for Chinese porcelain spread over the next century. It was *the* thing to have; high quality items were being imported more cheaply and frequently from Korea, though it soon became evident that it was high time to make it in Japan.

The shogun Toyotomi Hideyoshi made his second attempt to invade Korea in 1592. The campaign was disastrous, but to his general Nabeshima Naohige (among others) feudal lord of the old province of Hizen (now Saga Prefecture, Western Kyushu) Hideyoshi had given a 'license to trade', not in ceramics, but in the Korean potters themselves. "If there are persons skilled in ceramics found whilst encamped in Korea," went the shogun's instructions, "bring them back to Japan."

The Nabeshimas kept their potters in captivity, though what had initially been coercion became more a matter of keeping professional secrets from rivals. Perhaps as a reaction to

the ostentatious aficionados of porcelain, tea masters meanwhile came to prize the rough-hewn quality of stoneware all the more. Korean potters began by bringing subtle improvements to the same, notably in Karatsu; there was no clay suitable for porcelain in Japan anyway.

In 1616, the great Korean potter Li Sanpei discovered kaolin, the exceptionally light clay needed to provide porcelain with its whiteness and hardness, near the town of Arita. Working thenceforth from their 'secret kilns', the reclusive and exclusive Nabeshima potteries dominated the ceramics industry until the end of the feudal era.

In 1675 the potters moved from Arita to Okawachiyama, on the inland side of the port of Imari. This is how this kind of porcelain got its name—but not among the Japanese, who still prefer to call it Arita-yaki.

Early Imari was mainly blue and white, but, during the Kan'ei era (1624–43), the great ceramicist Sakaida Kakiemon introduced over-glaze enamelling. The concept was Ming dynasty Chinese, but the polychrome designs were inspired from Japanese textiles, lacquerware and screen paintings. With the collapse of the Ming dynasty in 1644, China's exports of blue and white porcelain virtually ceased. Meeting the booming European demand for it

provided the Japanese with a bonanza. Imari ware, both the polychrome enamel and the blue, were brought to Europe exclusively by the Dutch—the only foreigners apart from the Chinese allowed to trade on Japanese territory after 1639. Blue and white Imari proved highly influential in Holland, particularly in Delft, as well as in England and Germany. By the mid 17th century, Arita kilns were also producing European-style dinner services, often embellished with family crests. Porcelain was no longer a rarity in Japan and even the common people used it for soba noodle cups.

Today's connoisseurs use the term 'Old Imari' to distinguish from Imari—which now means anything made after a heyday lasting from the 1640s to the 1750s. During the 19th century Imari's reputation declined with mass-produced, stencilled designs often catering overmuch to the over-ornateness favoured by the European bourgeoisie. That said, potteries in the area nonetheless produced some outstandingly beautiful ceramics. Potteries in Okawachiyama and Arita continued to turn out traditional hand-painted Imari designs, as indeed they still do. Declared 'Intangible Cultural Assets' by the Government, the descendants of the Nabeshima and Kakiemon pottery families are still working there today.

Teaburi

手焙り
hand warmers

Time was when the Japanese believed that some creatures—foxes especially—could turn into human beings and wreak mischief. The dual concept of gods or men assuming animal form (zoomorphism) or of animals assuming human form (anthropomorphism) has at some time or other been the stuff of fairy tales, myth and religion all over the world. Zoomorphic ancient Egyptian and Hindu gods are legion; western folklore abounds with tales of witches turning themselves or others into animals. Most of the latter are sinister; none of the former could be properly described as cuddly. The cute factor would seem to be more recent. There are capitals in 12th-century French churches carved with many charming renditions of animals, but the charm is incidental or accessory. When it comes to really cute animals—especially walking on their hind legs, the West had to wait for Beatrix Potter in the 19th century. Japanese naturalist painters and *netsuke* carvers (not to mention makers of incense burners and even handwarmers) had been depicting animals and birds as cute for far longer than that, even though they remained mainly on four feet.

Nonetheless, having bunnies standing on their hind legs and going about human affairs may be perhaps a Japanese first. This emerges in one of the world's most charming and certainly earliest examples of using animals as caricatures of human beings. Kept in Kōzanji temple in Kyoto, this is the 12th-century Chōjūgiga (animal cartoon), a painted scroll attributed to the Buddhist priest Kakuyū (1053–1140) better known by his nickname Toba Sojō. It appears to illustrate a story about a competition umpired mainly by monkeys and foxes, culminating in a wrestling match between a rabbit and a victorious frog.

In China as in Japan, the depiction of animals is often tied to the Zodiac and the twelve beasts each ascribed to a particular year: rat, ox, tiger, hare, dragon, snake, horse, goat, monkey, rooster, dog and boar. The Japanese send New Year greeting cards depicting the annual animal; they often buy effigies of the same either for themselves or as gifts. At the end of the year, the horse that pranced atop the television set or the mouse that simpered on the kitchen cabinet will be relegated to the closet for another 12 years—or will wind up on the shelves of the local junk shop. Even a century ago, a handwarmer in the shape of a rabbit would have made a fine gift for the Year of the Hare.

From the early 20th century, the proliferation of cute, cuddly anthropomorphic animals has been been even more varied and rapid in Japan than elsewhere. You can even find cute renditions of animals that were never cute at all, including cuddly toys of dragons and snakes. Zoomorphism and anthropomorphism go over the top in Japan, where instruction manuals often depict electronic appliances with human faces. Cute is big business. 1999 was a boom year for Miffy, a bunny originally devised for books for small children by a Dutch illustrator in 1955, but which became an icon for teenage girls and grown women in Japan from the early 1970s. Not to be outdone, the Sanrio toy company soon came up with another rabbit, My Melody, and devised Hello Kitty, the feline equivalent (though not a zodiacal animal) of similar vintage.

Handwarmers never were big in Japan; and these days no one uses them at all. Instead they use Pokaron—a bag made of paper fabric and containing chemicals that heat up on contact with air. More than for warming hands, Pokaron and its countless spin-offs are for deep-heating aches and pains.

Hanakago

花籠
flower baskets

Whereas taste in the West was increasingly towards ostentatiousness in the 19th century, the Japanese cherished restraint and simplicity. One of the fields that exemplifies this is flower arranging. In the West, this mostly consisted of dropping a bulky, heterogeneous bunch of plants into a vase at random; in Japan it meant carefully choosing a minimal number of stems and blooms, before cutting and placing them in a suitable receptacle. At its most refined this was (and still is) *ikebana*—flower arrangement as an art form in its own right.

"To anyone of taste," American Japanologist Edward Morse lamented in the 1880s, "it is unnecessary to show how inappropriate our gilt and often brilliantly coloured flower-vases are for the objects they hold." He noted that the Japanese preferred to use vases with simple shapes, made of materials such as stone, with a deliberately rough finish. They favoured the kind of clay used in the West for jugs and roof-tiles; the subdued result perfectly offset the delicacy of the blooms and, moreover, the vases were often heavy enough to support an item such as a branch of a flowering cherry. "The Japanese make the most fascinating and appropriate flower-vases," he concluded, "but their potters are artists and, alas, ours are not!"

Nor did Morse confine his admiration only to ceramics. There were planed and polished wooden wall brackets made from a thin section of a tree-branch, upon which roughly cut branches were affixed in such a way that they could hold a couple of small planters. The carpenters who generally made buckets and sake barrels also made tiered wooden planters able to accommodate pots of different sizes. There were hundreds of varieties of wooden and bamboo plant holders: bamboo vases made for hanging from the pillars inside the house and rectangular vases of lacquered wood with a copper lining. Some of these items were so cheap that they were to be found in the most humble Japanese homes.

Among these alternatives for displaying flowers in Japan, he mentions *hanakago* (flower baskets), which are probably even more prominent today than they were then. Made mainly though by no means exclusively of bamboo, *hanakago* incorporate wood from roots and creepers into their manufacture and come in an astonishing variety of shapes and sizes. With just a few notable exceptions, until the end of the 19th century, the majority of craftsmen making *hanakago* were anonymous. With the growth of the Mingei movement (the Japanese equivalent of the British Arts &

Crafts Movement) during the 1920s, *hanakago* artisans grew in number and in reputation. Some of the finest (and most expensive) examples of *hanakago* on the antiques market date from about this time.

The material acquires a reddish brown to black patina—often assisted with lacquering. When not purely functional, *hanakago* were mainly made for *ikebana*—especially for flower decorations accompanying the tea ceremony (see pages 134–137). Craftsmen making *hanakago* also made other tea ceremony requisites, especially utensil boxes. Currently, *hanakago* artisans often produce remarkably sculptural, sometimes totally abstract works, which belong very much in the realm of contemporary fine art, and several have been designated 'Living National Treasures'.

Ishidōrō

石灯籠
stone lanterns

Amongst Japan's traditional crafts, *sekizai-gyō* (stone masonry) is a poor relation. You never seem to find the official rank of 'Living National Treasure' or 'Intangible Cultural Asset' bestowed upon *ishiku* (stone masons). Perhaps this is because of their overwhelmingly formulaic approach to stone-carving. Comprising figures for Buddhist temples, Shintō shrines, commemorative and funerary monuments and garden statuary, the scope of their output is pretty vast. Yet each follows a template. Standing in rows in the stone mason's yard, the statues of the Bodhisattva Kannon or Jizō (see pages 118–119), or each of the Seven Gods of Good Luck, are absolutely identical. The lion-dogs seated at the entrance to the Shintō shrine are always the same open-mouthed Ah and the closed-mouthed counterpart Un. Those sinister seated foxes, messengers of Inari, the deity of the hearth and harvest, always seem cloned. Even allowing for the fact that, in Japan's traditional culture, the lines of distinction between art and craft are almost non-existent, stone masonry is about as far removed from art as bricklaying.

Yet there are still subtle differences of style and flights of the imagination varying from one workshop to another. Also, given Japan's damp climate, many of those things

will—if left alone—grow moss and lichen and, perhaps with the unwelcome assistance of acid rain, acquire the patina of centuries in just a few years. Among the most beautiful of such objects are those made specially for the garden—above all the *tsukubai* or garden basin (see overleaf) and the *ishidōrō*—the stone lantern.

Although primarily for gardens, like much of the stone mason's repertoire, the *ishidōrō* are not entirely without religious or funerary connotations. They are connected with Obon, a seasonal festival lasting from mid July to mid August. A month-long equivalent of All-Souls or Hallowe'en, Obon is when the spirits of ancestors are said to return to earth. The season naturally inspires a wealth of ghostly tales but, far from being gloomy, it occasions dancing and fireworks at the height of the summer holidays.

The souls of the dead are often represented as flames in Japanese iconography. Thus, many temple festivals connected with Obon are 'lantern festivals'. Obon is a Buddhist festival, but also observed around Shintō shrines. Nara's famous Kasuga shrine, for instance, has 2,000 stone lanterns along the shrine approach—donated by devotees for almost a millennium. Another spectacular

show of stone lanterns is on the island of Miyajima near Hiroshima, where the lights similarly flicker twice a year in their little roofed towers of stone all along the coastal approach to Itsukushima shrine.

The most evocative stone mason's yard I saw was in the alpine Kiso valley. In addition to the usual, they make rough-hewn stone plaques called *reijin-no-hi*, believed by millions of devotees of a Shintō mountain cult to be the ticket to paradise. Having been invited by the stone mason and his family to shelter from a spectacular thunderstorm, I took tea with them around an *irori* fireplace (see pages 28–29). The grandmother was nursing an injured cat; he had been attacked, she said, by a fox—always a magical animal in Japan. When the sun came out again, golden droplets of water fell from the eaves of the house; the rows of glistening *ishidōrō* in the yard shone liked burnished brass. I could hear the whisper of the kettle on the hearth and the purring of the cat as I looked out over the yard. A huge rainbow seemed to emanate from a cluster of *reijin-no-hi* standing just beyond, and the eerie light shone on hundreds of thousands more stones set among the pines all the way up the mountainside.

Chōzubachi

手水鉢
water basins

You must have seen pictures even if you have never seen the real thing: a rough-hewn stone basin with maple-leaves or cherry-blossom petals floating in the water, which often tends to reflect the sky and surrounding greenery. Associated almost universally with the Japanese garden, the *chōzubachi* is a great favourite with photographers both home-grown and from overseas. There will most often be a water-dipper lying across it, the receptacle at the end consisting of a cylinder of bamboo or a small metal bowl. There will usually be a scattering of stones and pebbles around the base suggesting a miniature rockery; perhaps some moss or potted plants. Seeing it near the veranda of a traditional house or outside a hut for the tea ceremony, it would be hard indeed not to fall under its delicate aesthetic spell, but the obvious question is— what's it for?

Given that it is outdoors and thus could arguably be compared with the western bird-bath, it couldn't be designed for drinking from, surely? No, indeed. The scholar Edward Morse, residing in Japan during the late 1870s, had no doubt asked the same question. "A curious evidence of the cleanly habits of the Japanese is seen in the *chōzubachi*," he wrote, "a receptacle for water at the end of the veranda near the latrine. This convenience is solely for the purpose of washing the hands."

Even now that the adjoining out-house has been replaced by the indoor toilet for over a century, the *chōzubachi* endures (even though it is increasingly called a *tsukubai*, a term that has no connotations with the toilet). Writing specifically at the time in *Japanese Homes and their Surroundings*, Morse omitted to mention that *chōzubachi* are not just located near latrines, but invariably also are found in the grounds of shrines and temples, even though there is almost always a much larger equivalent with whole rows of water-dippers to accommodate several people. This speaks volumes for just how very much cleanly habits matter in Japan.

Emerging from pre-history, long before Buddhism arrived in Japan almost 1,500 years ago, the Shinto religion lays great emphasis on purity, and hence water is of primordial significance in its rituals. For example there is usually a *chōzubachi* just outside the side entrance of a Shintō shrine, especially if it adjoins a wedding hall. As they file in to take their seats for the ceremony, participants must pour water over their hands and rinse out their mouths—even if they have already done so at the main fountain standing on the shrine compound.

Japanese Buddhist temples incorporate many elements of Shintō origin, the *chōzubachi* being one of them. No Zen temple garden would ever be without one; for a tea ceremony, participants similarly purified themselves before entering the hut. And by the way, to prevent our feathered friends from mistaking the *chōzubachi* for a bath or worse, either the water is changed just before use or, as is the case with the larger water fountains, the receptacle has a roof over it. And if it doesn't, as is often the case in Japanese gardens today, it is because its function has become purely decorative.

Bonsai Basami

盆栽鋏
bonsai shears

A Japanese government survey on leisure recently put gardening as the nation's seventh most popular pastime. In a country in which 77 percent of the population is concentrated in small living spaces in large towns, the fact there are some 36 million amateur gardeners is surprising. Parkland may be found wanting but, thanks to the profusion of pots outside houses and on the balconies of apartment buildings, Japan's big cities are greener than they first seem. There is evidence of intensive gardening in every residential neighbourhood, with the cultivation of both flowering plants, and a variety of vegetables.

Of these, the bonsai tree—the Japanese miniature tree—stands out. Bonsai are by now universally known, but 19th-century visitors to Japan were very impressed. "It is very curious to see a sturdy old pine tree," remarked one, "masculine and gruff in its gnarled branches and tortuous trunk, perhaps 40 or 50 years old, and yet not over two feet in height, and growing in a flower pot." Wired and twisted to stunt their growth and carefully pruned, bonsai trees are in fact sometimes as much as two centuries old. Bonsai enthusiasts are legion in Japan; exhibitions and competitions are regularly held, among other places, at town halls, temples and shrines.

One who won prizes at such functions in my old Tokyo neighbourhood was an old man who cultivated them in the little garden space he had outside his wooden house. He had beautifully shaped maple trees and pines; the

displays of diminutive blossoming plums and cherries in spring stopped passersby in their tracks. Kimono or *hanten* jacket, he always wore traditional clothes as he pruned, watered and tended assiduously, frowning with concentration as he worked. But he was also rather intimidating. A staunch patriot, he would fly an outsize Japanese flag over his house on national holidays, and was also a renowned expert on the Japanese sword. This is not as incompatible with bonsai as it sounds; a balance struck between martial violence and delicate aesthetics was one of the intrinsics of Japanese warrior culture.

The bonsai man always had the right tools for the job from *bonsai basami* (bonsai shears), to the tiny leaf-cutting scissors and special cutters for removing knots and trimming roots. These had samurai connotations too. When the carriage of swords was outlawed after the ousting of the samurai government in 1868, many swordsmiths turned to making knives, scissors and garden clippers. A lot of traditional ironmongery is made by smiths using the same techniques as for sword blades. In addition to scissors and carpenters' tools, today's output includes kitchen knives for the filleting and preparation of raw fish.

Possessions and Clothing

In the 19th century when Japan first opened up to the West, certain objects defined the Japanese. The hairstyles, the clothes, the objects they carried with them or the ones they used—in the eyes of visitors, these things added up to how the Japanese looked. Though men gave up the topknot and the sword ages ago and no one toggles portable medicine cases to their sash with a *netsuke*, the past still echoes with the kimono, the fan, the wrapping of a gift and the faint whisper of the calligraphy brush on paper.

Nihon-tō and Tsuba

日本刃と鍔
swords and sword guards

"The occupation of swordsmith," wrote Japanologist Lafcadio Hearn, "was in the old days the most sacred of crafts: he worked in priestly garb, and practised Shintō rites of purification while engaged in the making of a good blade. Before the smithy was then suspended the sacred rope of rice straw (*shimenawa*), which is the oldest symbol of Shintō. None even of his family might enter there, or speak to him; and he ate only of the food cooked with holy fire."

Samurai placed themselves at the top of the social hierarchy of the Edo period (1603–1868), followed by farmers, artisans and merchants. A swordsmith, however, continued to enjoy a much more privileged position than other artisans. The early 12th-century Emperor Toba was said to have been a master swordsmith himself. The samurai regarded the sword both as sacred and a family heirloom; offerings were frequently left before it in the home—especially before battle. It was known as the proverbial 'soul of the samurai'.

The sword is one of the three sacred objects used during the coronation of an emperor. The other two are the mirror and the jewel—the former made of bronze and the latter actually a necklace made of uncut stones shaped like teardrops. Unseen by anyone except emperors and high priests, these objects have been used for as long as have Shintō shrines (about 1,700 years). Examples found in Japan and dating back to the 3rd century AD imply that the sword would be straight, probably double sided, two-handed and of Chinese or Korean manufacture.

Korean smiths were active in Japan during the Nara period (710–794), though Amakuni, a master Japanese swordsmith living sometime in the mid 8th century, was reputedly the inventor of the more characteristic blade with its elegant curve and razor-edge. The *nihon-tō* took shape during the Heian era (794–1185), and is considered to have been perfected during the Kamakura period (1185–1333), though production levels and quality continued to soar during the long era of more or less perpetual civil war lasting until 1600.

Of exceptional flexibility and durability, the *nihon-tō* owes its quality to a special process involving the folding and refolding of the metal during forging, producing a cutting edge of unsurpassed hardness along the length of a blade of softer steel. Designed to protect the hand and often showing the most beautifully designed and executed metalwork, the *tsuba* or sword guard was often made by a different specialist. Made for swords but sometimes never fitted, in some cases *tsuba* have outlived the sword they once embellished.

Samurai would walk abroad wearing two swords: the long *daishō koshirae* and the *wazikashi*, its shorter companion piece. Merchants and artisans were also permitted to carry swords, but theirs had to be substantially shorter. After the Meiji restoration of 1868, their carriage became prohibited and swords swamped a burgeoning new antique market. Recognized as being of unrivalled quality and already very expensive during the 19th century, the Japanese sword now finds avid collectors all over the world.

There were five main centres of sword production in Japan, and some still survive. Master swordsmiths continue to make sublime blades for ceremonial and decorative use, but swords currently account only for a fraction of the output from extant workshops. Many are mainly forging superb kitchen knives prized by the exponents of Japanese haute cuisine.

Kabuto

兜

samurai helmets

Seizing the popular imagination during the mid 20th century and exalted via a martial arts boom, the samurai (and their image above all) entered the realm of science fiction. Arch-villain of the Star Wars films, Darth Vader, owed his futuristic helmet and mask entirely to samurai battle wear. Out of all the armour of world history, the samurai concept was the most fantastic, and the warriors themselves are now the stuff of legend. But who were they?

Though they had existed in Japan long before, warriors came to the fore with the abrupt and violent end of the peaceful Heian era (794–1185), after which Japan was plunged into almost perpetual civil war for over 400 years. Having made the town of Kamakura his capital in 1185, the victorious war-lord Minamoto Yoritomo created a military government in which he ruled as shogun. Beneath him were the *daimyō* (literally 'big names'), who were regional governors with a warrior élite in their service. Called samurai (one-who-serves), these warriors became the aristocracy of a social system lasting nearly 700 years.

The Kamakura era ended in 1333, but subsequent governments fell many times during subsequent centuries marred by strife between regional clans. The ultimate goal was to unify the entire country. It was approached by Oda Nobunaga (1534–1582), neared by Toyotomi Hideyoshi (1536–1598) and reached by the shogun Tokugawa Ieyasu (1542–1616) after all rivals were crushed at the formidable battle of Sekigahara in 1600. Having founded the city of Edo (now Tokyo) in 1603, Ieyasu was father to the shoguns of the Tokugawa dynasty, which ruled Japan until 1868. The samurai remained the ruling caste, but since the Edo period was peaceful their heyday was past. Nonetheless, they needed to maintain their image and kept metal craftsmen busy with the manufacture of swords and armour —much of it more opulent and fanciful than anything seen during the centuries of warfare.

Of Chinese design, early Japanese armour consisted mainly of metal plates in front and back. Armour for common foot soldiers was fairly primitive; but *yoroi* (armour) for the élite consisted principally of a magnificent tunic and skirt elaborately fashioned from hundreds of parallel horizontal rows of strips of iron linked by silk cords, with similarly contrived shoulder-pads, arm-pieces and leggings. Covering the nose and chin was an iron mask or *menpō*, usually representing a human face, often with whiskers. Armour later improved substantially —notably with the adoption during the 16th century of a Western-style breastplate.

By far the most spectacular element was the *kabuto* or helmet for the commanders. The best were ridged helmets with the bowl made up of between 12 and 64 plates, sometimes featuring hundreds of rivets. There was a neck-guard consisting of about four iron plates at the back like a hood, usually lacquered for additional hardness. Atop the bowl there was an outsize forecrest, perhaps representing a skewed crescent moon, deer antlers, crab-claws or flames, often over 60 cm (2 ft) high. The *kabuto* was frequently crafted like a sculpture, representing perhaps an ancient lacquered court cap or the elongated (and distinctly phallic) bald head of old Fukurokuju, a god of good luck.

Hanten or Happi

半纏、法被
workmen's jackets

Rickshaw drivers, tradesmen, carpenters and coolies—most of the men in vintage Japanese photographs wear what looks like a short coat or tunic with wide sleeves. Known as *hanten* or *happi*, it is made of thick cotton and dyed with indigo. On the back and lapels it bears mainly (but not exclusively) white decorations applied by a resist-dye method, consisting of lettering and a *mon* (family crest). Deep ultramarine when new, the hanten fades to a colour like worn denim, which it resembles—not least because it was the standard outfit for workmen—the plebeian garb of old Edo.

Happi and *hanten* seem synonymous, though some argue the former applies only to livery denoting that the wearer is an employee. Others say that the term *hanten* is currently used to distinguish between the genuine (now quite expensive) hand-crafted article and the garish and flimsy cotton or acetate equivalent, including the 'happi coat' popular with tourists.

During the sweltering summer the *hanten* was often left flapping open over just a loincloth. In winter it was worn belted with a narrow *obi* or sash (see pages 56–57) over an undershirt and britches reaching around knee level. The *hanten* can now be worn like this by women too; until the 1950s it was a garment for men only.

Essentially a trade uniform, the *hanten* is still worn today, among others by market stall holders, traditional shopkeepers and staff in Japanese restaurants. You can also wear it over your jeans. Then as now, the *mon* on the back denotes membership of a company, guild or indeed, a *yakuza* gang. The *hanten* comes out in force for Shintō festivals. During Tokyo's colossal Sanja Matsuri in May, for instance, the custom is for each neighbourhood to carry ornate (and heavy) portable shrines through the streets, with both male and female bearers wearing *hanten* backed with the logo of the stores or associations they belong to.

Good antique *hanten* can fetch high prices, especially rarities such as those outwardly plain and richly patterned within. This custom originated with the sumptuary laws imposed at intervals during the Edo period (1603–1868), which forbade merchants and plebeians any display of luxury, especially with clothing. Wealthier merchants took to having kimono made in plain, dark colours with fabulously embroidered and/or handpainted linings. With this trend, members of the populace followed suit. Even if you could only afford to wear cotton or hempen cloth, you could always flash a fancy lining to impress your peers.

This applied particularly to *hanten* worn by firemen. In an era of wooden houses and frequent fires, firemen or *tobi* were regarded as the most dashing figures in all *shitamachi* (low city; the plebeian quarter of Edo). Underneath the bland exterior of their *hanten* were fantastic coloured prints of mythical heroes fighting demons and dragons, which they additionally believed would bring them luck in their dangerous profession. In fact, they reserved this kind of finery only for Dezome-shiki, their annual parade. Featuring astonishing balancing feats conducted atop poles and ladders, the festival is still held each January in Tokyo, but nowadays any decoration on their *hanten* will only be on the outside.

Kimono

着物
kimono

Japan boasts what is probably the world's most distinctive traditional costume. Celebrated in western 19th-century pictorial and operatic fantasies, the kimono (wearing-thing) graces the contemporary cat-walk; it never really goes out of fashion. Though it has always changed according to the vagaries of seasonal trends, the basic design remains much the same as it was when it first emerged some 400 years ago.

In pre-medieval Japan, clothing was of Sino-Korean inspiration. The Japanese passion for fashion really took off during the Heian era (792–1185), when courtiers of both sexes began competing sharply to out-dress each other. The textiles accordingly grew more elaborate, but the designs gradually simplified —perhaps due to practical considerations; spawned by almost 500 years of intermittent civil war, warlords and their families were often on the move. During the calmer Edo period (1603–1868), the kimono found its definitive form, albeit with much longer sleeves and a hem trailing on the ground. Above all, the kimono's development and proliferation came about with the rise of a moneyed merchant class and remarkable progress made in textile printing and dyeing techniques.

Within the categories of formal, semi-formal and casual, the variety of kimono is virtually infinite. With the exception of summer variants, however, the term 'casual' hardly applies. Coming in more subdued tones, but with great intricacy of weave and extreme refinement of fabrics, 'casual' kimono can be even dearer than the ceremonial varieties. After all, *shibui* (sober refinement) stands as the paradigm of Japanese aesthetics. Fabrics reflecting these would be used for *tomesode*, the short-sleeved kimono worn by married women, but rarely in the *furisode*, a brightly patterned kimono with long, baggy sleeves worn by unmarried women. In cooler weather, the kimono can be worn with a *haori*, a coat typically made of unadorned coloured silk.

With a spectrum comprising mainly blue, brown, black or white and an intermittent range of greys—the male kimono is more sober. A man's formal kimono is black, adorned only with a small family crest printed outside the lapels, on the back and on each sleeve. A grey striped skirt called a *hakama* completes the picture. A component of the traditional bridegroom's costume, the *hakama* is also worn (nowadays by both sexes) for martial arts such as archery and *kendo* and by girls at university graduation ceremonies. In the 1870s when Western dress was adopted, men wore kimono much more rarely than women.

The *yukata* is a light cotton kimono worn by both sexes in summer, and often used as sleep-wear all year round. It is traditionally white with a dark blue pattern, but in recent years women have been wearing *yukata* with much bolder colours and designs, especially during summer festivals. There are juvenile kimono for both sexes, worn especially during the annual Shichi-Go-San (3-5-7) festival, when children of those ages receive blessings at the local Shintô shrine.

Obi

帯

kimono sashes

The adult kimono comes in one size, the extra length being folded up at the waist and held in place by a silk sash called *obi*, the female variant being gorgeously decorated, typically of silk brocade. Both of very simple design, a kimono and *obi* can be made in a single day, but the material can take months to produce.

Kimono fabrics are mostly decorated using stencils or elaborate resist-dye methods. Three of the most famous are brightly coloured Bingata from Okinawa and Yuzen, most prevalent in Kanazawa and Kyoto, where it is said to have been invented by a 17th-century painter, and Shibori, an intricate tie-dyed fabric. Involving as many as 100,000 dots, each is made by twisting thread around a tiny, bunched piece of material. Hand-woven fabrics are sometimes made by artisans who have given their fingernails a serrated cut specially to rake back the strands of silk. Tapestry and embroidery techniques are frequently used in the kimono, but preponderantly in the *obi*. Although embroidery is now mainly confined to enhancing the designs with gold and silver thread (as in Kyoto's famous Nishijin brocade), wholly embroidered textiles do still exist. There are textile artists active today through-out the country, and some of the more famous command astronomical prices. Small wonder

that even very high quality textiles are now mainly made and printed by machine, often programmed by computer.

Men's *obi* are of a width averaging 10 cm (about four inches), but the female variety is about 3.6 m (12 ft) long by 30 cm (12 in) wide and tied with an outsize bow at the back. Through the ages the *obi* has varied in style and thickness. Once upon a time it was tied in front, a fashion dying out on the eve of the 17th century—when it came to be the preserve of and signifier for prostitutes. Shigasaki, for instance, a top courtesan during the 1770s, is said to have broken all *obi* records with an example over 80 cm (30 in) wide. She was accordingly nicknamed Obi-Shigasaki or, more unkindly, Obi-gokumon. The *gokumon* (prison gate) was where the heads of criminals were exposed after execution—inferring that Shigasaki's *obi* was so broad that only her head was visible above it.

Since the 1900s Western women have affected wearing the kimono as a dressing gown—without *obi*—something which never fails to raise Japanese eyebrows. The kimono is hardly leisure wear in Japan. Many women resort to dressers from beauty-parlours when they need to wear one. Worn over an under kimono, the outer kimono often needs to be

specially padded to hang correctly. Requiring additional silk cords, an *obi* can take around half an hour to tie; most of today's women are unable to do it themselves. The *obi* is pretty constricting and the kimono tight around the rump. The *zōri*, the elegant little sandals worn with it, command a pigeon-toed, narrow-stepped gait (see page 63). All this makes the kimono highly impractical for the office and rush-hour travel. It is now mainly reserved for ceremonies such as university graduation, weddings and funerals, as well as New Year shrine visits and formal family gatherings. Kimono are worn also by staff in more traditionalistic shops, restaurants and bars, as well as by the constantly dwindling geisha.

Nonetheless, apart from rural grannies who have worn them all their lives, there are women who still wear kimono every day—if they can afford to. In all events, the pattern and colour of the kimono fabric must match the season and the occasion—so that even in humbler Japanese households, most women still own more than one.

Netsuke and Ojime

根付と緒締

toggles and cord tighteners

It may be elegant, but the kimono has never had pockets. Mostly donning it only for an hour or two at a wedding, funeral or when everyone dresses up Japanese-style over the New Year, men put their requisites away either in the capacious sleeves or inside the folds—hoping that the belt will hold them. Wearing kimono more often, women now carry matching handbags. During the heyday of the kimono, however, the amount of paraphernalia a man had to carry around was considerable. He had a purse, keys, a tobacco pouch (the weed was introduced to Japan by the Portuguese in the 16th century), pipe-case and an *inrō* (a miniature medicine chest) (see pages 70–73), not to mention such oddments as a small travelling writing case comprising brush and ink (see page 77). These items were called *sagemono* (hanging things), for they were hung from the *obi* or kimono sash (see pages 56–57) using a kind of toggle

to stop them falling off. In the 15th century, the fashion was toward small polished gourds. Those with much to carry often had several gourds at their waists, from whence there dangled an unsightly clutter running very much counter to Japanese aesthetic principles.

The answer to the *sagemono* problem came with the *netsuke*—a small toggle made specially for hanging it from the *obi*. The drawstring attaching the *sagemono* to the *netsuke* was passed through a bead called an *ojime* which, plain or decorated, generally matched the *netsuke*. Appearing sometime

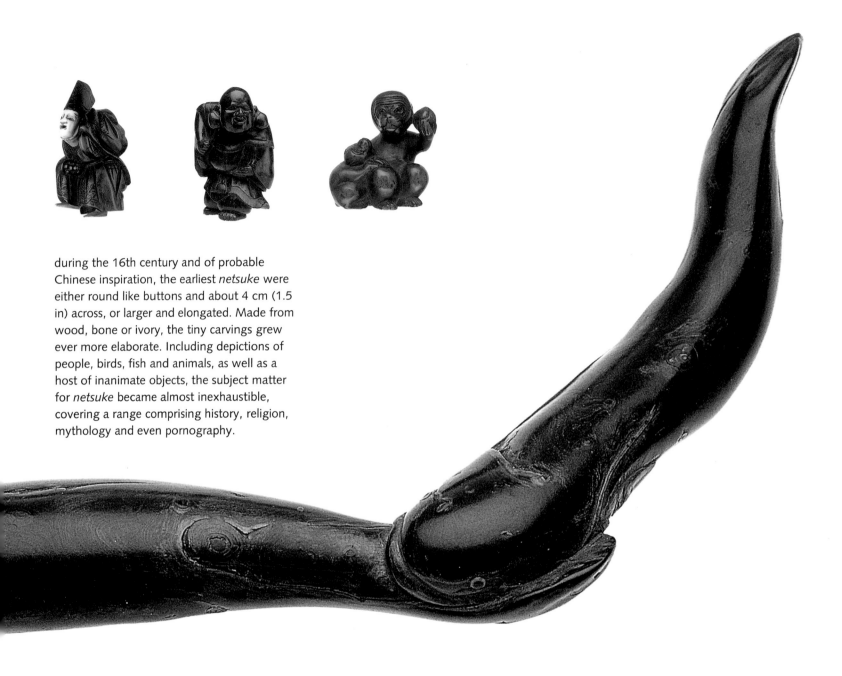

during the 16th century and of probable Chinese inspiration, the earliest *netsuke* were either round like buttons and about 4 cm (1.5 in) across, or larger and elongated. Made from wood, bone or ivory, the tiny carvings grew ever more elaborate. Including depictions of people, birds, fish and animals, as well as a host of inanimate objects, the subject matter for *netsuke* became almost inexhaustible, covering a range comprising history, religion, mythology and even pornography.

Though it is known that they came to supplant gourds, the form in which *netsuke* really came into being is still a matter of scholarly debate. Chinese origin has been ruled out, but not entirely. Some experts believe that a form of *netsuke*, imported from China, existed as early as the 13th century, but was used only for hanging keys. Meanwhile there were many small trinkets imported from China, especially seals made of wood and ivory, often beautifully carved. It seems likely that at some point someone simply drilled a hole through one of these and used it as a toggle—the anonymous instigator of a craze which began early in the 17th century, when Japan's carvers of wood, bone and bamboo as well as lacquer artisans began making *netsuke* of their own.

A book about the Japanese collection in London's British Museum places *netsuke* under "Secular Sculpture" which, strange as it seems, is apt. The Japanese propensity for miniaturization goes back much further than the personal stereo, and *netsuke*, which are probably about as old as the bonsai tree, can frequently be sculptural masterpieces. As Western visitors to Japan noted from the 1860s, outside of religious edifices, Japan was not much given to sculpture. Men seemed to be wearing the secular variety on their belts. Having already reached its zenith during the ostentatious 18th century, the artistry of *netsuke* attracted foreign collectors almost immediately. By the 1900s they were top of the list of hot souvenirs and—if by a known master—could be dauntingly expensive.

Meanwhile, as the majority of men took to wearing Western suits to work during the Meiji era (1868–1912), *netsuke* dwindled in the wake of a plethora of pockets and the advent of the briefcase. Japanese carvers were soon making *netsuke* mainly for the Western market. Unfortunately, many *netsuke* masters also turned to making larger pieces in the same materials, with predictable lapses in aesthetic standards. In the late 19th century, the troupe of elephants carved out of a single tusk, or the group of girlies in kimonos, came to be complemented with equivalents in bronze.

With astronomical prices paid by Japanese and international collectors today (US$10,000 is not unusual for an outstanding piece), the market for tiny *netsuke* has rarely been brisker. Predictaby, the trade in fakes (made in China and Hongkong as well as Japan) continues to thrive—and has done for well over 100 years. Unless machine-tooled, however, really good fakes can only be made by master carvers—many of whom legitimately make reproductions which, even as such, can still command astronomical prices.

Hakimono

履物
traditional footwear

There is no shortage of trendy Japanese shoe designers and any number of students studying to become one in art colleges in Japan; millions of chic shoes are purchased by millions of Japanese. But far from the big-name fashion stores in the city centre, every neighbourhood has a cheap shoe-store which tells you much about what the Japanese really like to put on their feet. The variety is staggering.

There are canvas shoes, leather shoes, Chinese kung-fu slippers, galoshes, rubber boots, sneakers and trainers. There are plastic slippers for wearing on the way to the toilet and others to be donned while actually in it; there are different kinds of slippers for wearing in the house, but emphatically not on the tatami mats. There are remedial sandals with knobs of plastic and magnetized metal for massaging the feet while you stand or walk. There are also *jika-tabi*, a kind of split-toed, rubber-soled canvas boot worn by workmen. Then there are dainty *zōri*, ladies' sandals for wearing with a kimono, which are made of leather or fabric, with a thong between the toes. An odd variant is the *pokkuri* (see right) which has a sole about 10 cm (4 inches) high. A century ago, high-class courtesans used to go on an annual parade on *pokkuri* 30 cm (almost a foot) high.

The Y-shaped, between-the-toe configuration typifies that great, now little worn Japanese classic with both male and female variants: the *geta*, a wooden sandal with high supports. Until the 1950s, there was also a version rain-proofed with a leather upper, which perhaps explains why these sandals are still sometimes referred to as 'clogs'. And let us not forget *setta*, another thonged sandal, usually with woven rushes or tatami matting on a rubber sole. There might even be hybrid configurations of all or any of these, which is really rather strange—because the Japanese don't really like shoes at all.

Outdoor shoes of any persuasion are an absolute no-no in bath-houses, traditional Japanese inns, restaurants with tatami mats, religious buildings and homes. Before entering such an interior, guests leave shoes in lockers or the floor of the entrance hall. Walking shod over tatami mats is a kind of sacrilege. "From the nature of this soft-matted floor, shoes are never worn upon it," explained Edward Morse in 1880, "the Japanese invariably leave their wooden clogs outside the house, either on the stepping-stones or on the earth-floor at the entrance. The wearing of shoes in the house is one of the many coarse and rude ways in which a foreigner is likely to offend these people."

Boot-heels could not only leave indentations on the matting, he said, but even break right through. Happily, he concluded: "The act of removing one's shoes on entering the house is one of the very few customs that foreigners recognise—the necessity of compliance being too obvious to dispute." This is as true today as it was over a century ago; even in Western-style carpetted wall-to-wall apartments, shoes stay in the entrance hall.

Take a look at the shoes discarded in the average entrance way of an apartment or house. Women's shoes are always kept impeccable, but the men's—in working class or rural neighbourhoods—have the backs trodden down, the fronts scuffed. Real men don't wear shoes; they wear *geta*. Men with shiny shoes are married and/or urbanites, the upkeep of their shoes being undertaken either by their wives or those elderly shoe-shiners you see outside train stations. The reality is that many people have still not quite got used to shoes.

Western clothing was decreed the norm for office wear for men in 1872. That meant a three-piece suit with a *hai-karā* (high collar), the word coined for the detachable, starched contrivance at the neck of the *wai-shatsu* (white shirt). All of these things were often cited at the time as being uncomfortable, but none so much as the shoes. Though debatably honoured with a real Japanese word, shoes remain rather suspect. Unlike *geta*, they are made of leather—skin from dead animals. *Hakimono* means footwear, but to non-Japanese footwear it hardly applies. Shoes are alien things and called *kutsu*—written with characters meaning 'changed leather'.Western shoes—first

manufactured domestically in 1870 in Tsukiji, a district of Tokyo—took a long time to be accepted in Japan and made available in shoe stores.

Like the shoe-shiners outside the stations, the shoestore owner may also be a cobbler. Some of them would be members of a group who descended from an ancient pariah caste. Although this is fortunately diminishing, they still suffer a degree of discrimination in Japanese society. The problem lies in ancient Buddhist prescriptions against killing animals or eating meat. Thus while everyone eats meat and wears or uses leather, they have for centuries been shunning the butchers and tanners catering to them as an under-class.

But the one thing those shoe stores are least likely to stock is *waraji*—a straw sandal now rarely worn except by Buddhist temple pilgrims (see right). Several temples in Japan have giant versions as a decoration, made of woven rushes and measuring over six feet in length. At Ishiteji temple on Shikoku island, elderly people and arthritics tie pairs of *waraji* on the kind of rack reserved for *ema* (see pages 114–115), believing that this will keep them walking as long as possible. Many of these need to; they are on Shikoku's

renowned Buddhist pilgrimage, which embraces 88 temples. Most in fact now do the trip in buses, which is just as well, since *waraji* wear out in no time.

However pious the connotations of *waraji*, they still stay outdoors. In some Buddhist countries it is rude to sit in such a way as to show others the soles of your feet—shod or not. The ground is impure, and feet and shoes are polluted for being in contact with it. This might explain why Japanese ghosts have no feet; fading from the waist down, they narrow into a vapour trail. Perhaps in death they are spared the indignity of contact with the ground. They are thus relieved of the trouble of taking shoes on and off before entering and leaving the house—and of wearing plastic slippers in the toilet.

Kushi and Kanzashi

櫛と簪
traditional combs and hair ornaments

"In the street one sees the most poorly dressed girls with their hair beautifully arranged," Edward Morse noted in the 1880s, "Even little children, four or five years old, will often show that more care is taken with their hair than with their dress, which may even be ragged. A tousled head is not a common sight." The Japanese are fastidious. Standing in a crowded city street in post-industrial Japan, where rags are history, the passers-by are all attired pretty much as they would be in London or New York—but usually that much neater.

Women's hair is always sleek, glossy and, of course, black (though now brown or peroxide blonde, and sometimes even fuchsia or green). Japanese hair appears to remain black well into old age, but appearances are deceptive. Upon sighting the first strand of grey, legions of women and not a few men, unless nature first banishes hair altogether, reach for the dye bottle. Less a matter of personal vanity than one of public face, keeping up appearances is vital. Every city neighbourhood and even rural hamlets have at least one each of a barber and beauty salon. Apart from the fastidiousness, and the fact that a man's haircut can, following several shampooings and scalp massages, take over an hour, the hair styles look much as they do in the West. So,

are the strange (and often exorbitantly priced) hand-made combs and hair ornaments seen in the windows of certain traditional shops, used any more? Certainly. These *kanzashi* (hair ornaments), the pins and bodkins designed to grace the elaborate hairdos of centuries past, are very much part of contemporary life.

Like *kanzashi*, traditional Japanese combs (*kushi*) are often still made by hand. As they are intended for an extraordinary variety of hairstyles, they come in quite a variety of shapes. Single and doubled-edged combs, semicircular combs and square combs. There are others with long, sharp handles and a small toothed section which, sometimes cut at an angle, are for combing back hair at the sides of an elaborate traditional coiffure. These days they are likely to be used only by geisha and in all probability are used mainly for styling wigs. Combs are commonly made of boxwood, often beautifully carved and decorated, and frequently lacquered. They may also be made of tortoiseshell and/or inlaid with nacre and semi-precious stones.

Traditional hair styling goes with traditional attire. Though men have been largely exempt since the 1870s, many formal occasions still dictate the wearing of the kimono for women. Men generally discarded the kimono shortly

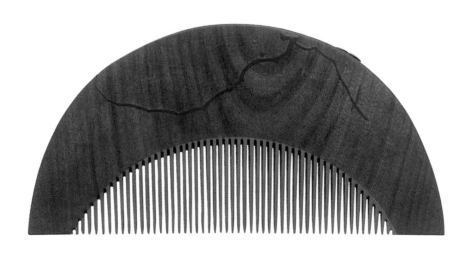

after they did their traditional hairstyle, which consisted of a tonsure complemented with a queue folded over the head. Emerging during the 16th century and worn first by the samurai, the style altered over the years according to changing fashions, but always required intricate shaping and shaving the head every three days. There was no shortage of barbers in pre-modern Japan, where women hairdressers regularly serviced all the female members of even modest households. Drawn back, folded, looped and bedecked with silk crêpe—women's elaborate hairstyles required fixing with much larger amounts of the same vegetable wax that men used for their topknots.

Still extant during the late 19th century, the most typical of these hairstyles was known as the Shimada, said to be named after Shimada Jinsuke, a celebrated 17th-century male geisha. Indeed, the principle harbingers of fashion in the Edo period were male players of female roles in the Kabuki, and high-class prostitutes known as Oiran.

J E DeBecker, British lawyer and ardent (though disapproving) student of Tokyo's Yoshiwara licensed quarter in the 1890s said of a courtesan's hairstyle: "It was a wonderful pyramidal coiffure ornamented with numerous tortoise-shell and coral hairpins so closely

thrust together as to suggest a halo of light encircling her head… she must indeed have been awe-inspiring and magnificent to the uninitiated." Although extravagantly embellished with the Oiran's outsized hairpins, this too would have been a form of Shimada coiffure. In vogue for some 200 years, the style saw a great deal of variants; it is the one most likely to be worn today by a geisha in full formal attire—as well as by the Japanese bride. Nowadays this kind of coiffure is worn overwhelmingly in the form of a wig.

The passing of these hairstyles altered Japanese sleeping habits both for men and women; designed to prevent the crushing of the coiffure and once ubiquitous, an uncomfortable wooden pillow with high supports disappeared unmourned. Gone too are the Oiran's huge hairpins, but a vast array of *kanzashi*, mainly designed to be worn with a kimono, are very much in use today.

"Here one sees the ingenious ways in which, with the simplest materials—cloth, gold paper, delicate spiral springs, straw, spangles, red coral, etc., a great variety of objects are made." So Edward Morse described *kanzashi* in the 1880s. "Quite half the designs represent flowers. Many of them represent a story or act of some kind; a child painting, a

birdcage, a bird in bamboo. Elaborate as some of them are, the cost is trifling." All his observations still apply, except for the latter. Good *kanzashi* are now made by a small number of craftsmen and incorporate precious metals. Never less than affordable, the prices can go up to the astronomic. The versions worn by women are generally simpler than the ones Morse describes, which are typically worn by little girls in ceremonial attire.

Craftsmen making combs are becoming rare; some have been put to work in museums. I recall meeting an old man in his workshop in a corner of a folk museum in the mountainous Kiso valley some 15 years ago. He asked me if I knew why the teeth of the traditional boxwood combs are so close together. "When the ladies styled their hair in the old days," he said with a mischievous grin, "They liked to comb the lice out at the same time." Since that time, the sleek coiffures on the willowy beauties in Japanese woodblock prints have never looked quite the same.

Inrō

印籠
medicine purses

A narrow little box with up to six tiered compartments, the *inrō* was devised especially for medicines. Originating early in the 16th century, it reached its apogee during the Edo period (1603–1868). Along with purses and smoking requisites, it was one of the *sagemono* (hanging things) habitually attached to the kimono sash. Reflecting the acme of miniature craftsmanship—in terms of lacquerware, carving, painting and often all three combined, fine *inrō* were very expensive. Merchants had them but, according to the shogunate sumptuary laws, they were not allowed to display them; samurai could display them but it was considered beneath their dignity to do so. So it isn't surprising that, kept mainly at home, they became collectibles early on in their history. By the 19th century, lacquerware producers were creating *inrō-dansu* (*inrō* chests) specially to accommodate a collection.

The exterior of *inrō* are variously painted with human figures, animals, sprigs of trees with birds and landscapes; the lacquered surfaces are frequently inlaid with designs made of precious woods, ivory or horn, tortoise-shell, pearl, gold, oxydized silver, coral and semi-precious stones. Even more extravagant, the insides of the boxes are sometimes lined with *nashiji* (aventurine lacquer) or silver or gold leaf. *Inrō* are also sometimes made of metal with cloisonné inlay.

Inrō specialists achieved considerable renown. Esteemed particularly for the quality and variety of their *inrō* throughout the Edo period, for example, the Kajikawa were an illustrious family of lacquerware producers in the employ of the shogunate. Their products tended to be more sober than the Shibayama, who rose to prominence in the latter half of the Edo period, as the merchant class grew wealthier and tastes became accordingly more ornate. Rarely to be found for less than US$800 and escalating sometimes to the lofty regions of US$80,000, *inrō* are as proportionately expensive today as they were when new.

Probably spurning the unsightly clutter of *sagemono* dangling around their waists, women mainly tucked items such as purses and *inrō* in their *obi*. *Inrō*, it seems, were more often used by men. Perhaps the same goes for the medicines they contained. The Japanese predilection for tonics is evidenced by their proliferation in pharmacies and in the ubiquitous street-side vending machines containing *herusu dorinku* (health drinks). Considered good antidotes to overwork and hangovers, the most common health drinks contain little more than vitamin C, sugar and lashings of caffeine but some include herbs from the old Sino-Japanese pharmacopoeia. A few pharmacies have acquired a certain renown for herbal powders and pills they have been preparing for over 200 years. Itōgan, for example, made in Tsuwano, Shimane prefecture, long ago boasted efficacy for an array of ailments (even leprosy); today it is sought as an antidote for over-indulgences in eating and drinking. The demand for medicines like these soars in modern Japan but, having gone into eclipse with the advent of clothes with pockets, the *inrō* was already history long before there were health drinks and vending machines.

Tabako

煙草
tobacco paraphernalia

"Smokin' Clean!" It's an oft seen slogan for a Japanese cigarette brand but, to people from nations trying to reduce health hazards posed by tobacco, it sounds like an oxymoron. In Japan, however, over a third of the population smoke—men accounting for nearly 60 percent. The weed is endorsed on billboards; non-smoking train carriages are a novelty and the smokeless zones in restaurants are few and far between. Although signs are that it is waning, as in most places, the Japanese love affair with tobacco is over 400 years old.

Blame it on the Portuguese. They introduced tobacco (along with muskets and sponge cake) when they landed in Japan in the 16th century. Enjoyed by both men and women of all social strata, the habit spread quickly over most of the country. However, ever wary of whatever gives pleasure to the populace, the shogunate soon prohibited it, but the ban was lifted in the 17th century.

Tobacco was smoked in a pipe called a *kiseru*, a word some experts believe implies Cambodian origin. The pipe itself was derived more from the European clay pipe which, with a long stem and fairly wide bowl, it at first resembled. However, like many things adopted and adapted in Japan, it underwent a miniaturization process—the bowl shrank down to become very small indeed. Typically, though there are variants, the *kiseru* has a metal bowl and mouthpiece connected by a long thin bamboo stem. Shorter stems are common, especially with ornamented *kiseru* entirely made of metal or ceramic. The short version of the *kiseru* was usually kept in a case, which was often beautifully decorated and held pride of place alongside the other *sagemono* dangling from the kimono sash.

Very finely shredded, the tobacco was kept in a pouch, which often also contained a lighting device using flint and steel. Like the case, the pouch was often finely decorative, typically being made of tooled leather. Other smoking requisites peculiar to Japan include a small tobacco tray, the *tabako bako* (tobacco box) formerly placed before guests and, most notably, the *hibachi* (see pages 30–31). Often set in a box containing drawers for tobacco paraphernalia, the *hibachi* was a portable brazier that came in handy as an outsize ashtray.

Tobacco production and sale became a Japanese state monopoly in 1904 and so remained until 1985—although the government still holds the lion's share of domestic tobacco companies. Shortly after the Meiji Restoration (1868), the Japanese turned to cigarettes and the *kiseru* began to die out.

Bunbōgu

文房具
traditional stationery

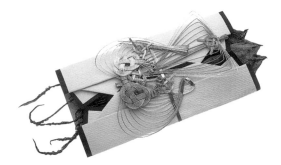

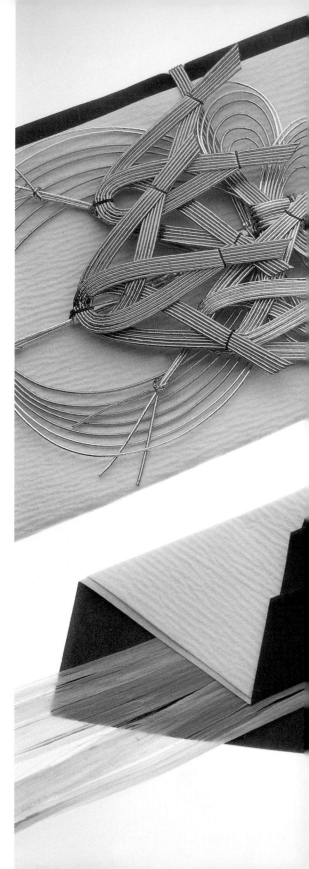

Most western visitors to Japan will be struck by just how different the *bunbōgu-ya* or stationery shop is from the equivalent back home. At first glance the notepaper, computer stationery, pens and pencils and so on seem familiar enough, but closer inspection soon reveals pointers to a wholly different cultural environment. For instance, there are many occasions when it is proper to make presents of money in Japan, but it is always extremely rude to hand it over just like that, so there's a whole range of variously sized and decorated envelopes specially conceived for the purpose —collectively known as *noshi bukuro*.

Such envelopes are invariably prettily secured with *mizuhiki*: special red and white (and silver and gold) paper string tied in decorative knots. Made even to represent birds and animals and using string of different colours, the knots are sometimes astonishingly elaborate. *Mizuhiki* is a craft in its own right.

Envelopes are needed for celebrating the arrival of a new baby and for *otoshidama*, the pocket money given to children at New Year. Then there is a tiny decorative envelope called *ôiri bukuro*, devised to contain a coin or two, which film and theatre companies offer staff as a token bonus when box office receipts exceed expectation. Though the custom is

now markedly waning, envelopes are essential for *yuinō*, the exchange of gifts between families of couples on the occasion of their engagement. Devised for gifts symbolically alluding to health, wealth, happiness, fertility and longevity, in addition to money, the envelopes contain dried foodstuffs (see right): seaweed and, most importantly *noshi* (paper-thin strips of abalone or squid), which is how the *noshi bukuro* got its name. The envelopes used at the wedding itself will contain money almost exclusively. Envelopes are also used at funerals (with black and white *mizuhiki* only), and those generally contain money too. Such ceremonies in Japan are elaborate and expensive; by making a contribution, relatives and participants share the cost.

The *bunbōgu-ya* also stocks, among the marker pens, a range of calligraphy brushes. There are magic marker versions, those that children use when learning to render *kanji* characters in black ink and the brushes used by adults for writing formal letters and seasonal greeting cards (notably for New Year). Serious calligraphy or Sho-dō (way of the brush) demands brushes of higher quality, as do artists practising traditional *suiboku-ga* (ink painting). Stationers sell handmade *washi* papers prepared from tree bark, often with

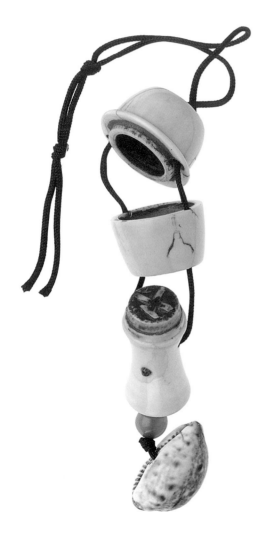

inclusions such as tiny leaves and flowers, petals, flecks of gold or silver leaf; they also sell coloured and patterned papers destined solely for origami. The larger the stationer, the larger the selection.

Some *bunbōgu-ya* specialize in Sho-dō requisites exclusively (don't even think of asking for fax paper); these are notably in Nara, renowned as a centre for brushes and *sumi* (ink tablets or sticks) for well over 1,000 years. Made of deer, horse, rabbit, squirrel or imported badger hair, brushes here are sized and shaped according to different applications. Made from the soot of bullrushes, the cakes of *sumi* in Nara may also be subtly coloured with natural dyes and even scented with musk; some of the manufacturers' formulas are secrets jealously guarded for generations.

A fine *bunbōgu-ya* also stocks *suzuri-bako* (*suzuri* is ink-stone; *bako* is box) or writing boxes (see right). Coming in different sizes, these are made of polished or lacquered wood—often lavishly decorated and priced accordingly—the cheaper items often made in China or Korea. The box contains partitions devised for the ink-stone, ink-stick and a small water dropper made of ceramic or metal. Shaped like a small pot, the dropper is for wetting the inkstone. You then rub with the inkstick until the desired intensity of black is achieved.

Almost all *bunbōgu-ya* have stands with racks containing row upon row of seals (see left). Introduced from China, they were in regular use in Japan from the 7th century. Arranged according to the order of the phonetic *hiragana* alphabet, seals cover all the most common family names: Kato, Sato, Suzuki, Yamamoto, and more—the Smiths and Joneses of Japan. Generically called *inkan*, seals are more commonly called *hanko* and most people have more than one. The *hanko* are for stamping ordinary business correspondence, invoices and receipts; more official and complex transactions are signed with a *jitsu-in*—a seal that must be registered in the local town hall. Then there are several other kinds: *mitome-in*, which is just a little more formal than the *hanko*, corporate seals and others used solely for banking.

A little over 5 cm (2 in) long, *inkan* are made of box-wood, bone or sometimes ivory or stone (for example, jade), and range in price from just a few hundred to well over 10,000 yen. They are carried in little leather containers with a silver clasp, lined with silk brocade and containing a small red ink-pad.

Furoshiki

風呂敷
cloth wrapping

When it comes to buying gifts in a Japanese airport, beware of the *furoshiki*. What you thought was a beautiful ladies' scarf transpires to be too short and thick when folded around the neck; what looked like a set of attractive handkerchiefs could only feasibly be used as such by an elephant. The *furoshiki* is often made of silk and may be elaborately tie-dyed or printed, sometimes even by hand. So it's easy to make a mistake; you had already heard that the Japanese consider blowing noses beyond the pale, an act imposing privacy and preferably perpetrated with a tissue. The handkerchiefs everyone seems to carry in Japan are really for drying the hands in public washrooms. Unlike *furoshiki*, they are overwhelmingly white.

Moreover, traditional Japanese and western design concepts and clothing styles are kept pretty rigorously apart, so that scarves with oriental motifs are the kind of thing that Westerners wear. They are most unlikely to be made in Japan, where scarf wearers prefer Versace and Dior. So the *furoshiki* isn't a scarf.

So, what is it? Above all, a *furoshiki* is used much as a carrier bag, notably for bearing gifts, which is strange, because it started life during the Edo period (1603–1868) as a bath-mat (*furo*: bath; *shiki*: mat, cover). It was a square of cloth, usually cotton, which people used to carry toilet requisites, towels and clothing to and from the public bathhouse. After the bath, they stood on it while they changed. It must have soon become apparent that it was handy for carrying lots of other things; even today you see people tying up the four corners of a *furoshiki* and carrying a great variety of objects. The sizes can vary a great deal; *furoshiki* more than 2 sq m (22 sq ft) are by no means unheard of; one sometimes sees them used, for instance, to wrap large drums used during Shintō festivals. I once saw one used to carry a small grandfather clock from an antique dealer's shop.

Presentation is vitally important in Japan, so that gift-wrapping has become an art form demanding skill in paper folding. The *furoshiki* eliminates the need for wrapping paper, but dictates rituals of its own. When you bring someone a gift in a *furoshiki*, it is customary to unwrap the latter yourself in front of the recipient before presenting it to them. Otherwise, it would be the height of rudeness. Since no one keeps anyone else's *furoshiki*, the recipient would assume that you expect something in return and would be obliged to put something into the *furoshiki* before giving it back to you.

Depending on what is being carried, there are also different ways of folding the *furoshiki* and tying its corners. There are special folding techniques for watermelon and other round, heavy objects as well as for square ones. Like the tying and folding used to ensure that two large sake bottles can be carried without knocking into each other, the techniques can be very ingenious.

Often more the stuff of obligation, reciprocation and the currying of favours than spontaneous generosity, gift-giving reaches a frenzy in Japan, especially during *setsubun* (the parting of the seasons) and at weddings. These occasions see the use of countless *furoshiki*, which explains why Japanese gift shops always sell them—including in airports.

Ōgi

扇
folding fans

During the stifling summer months in Japan, fans were eagerly sought by both men and women and still ubiquitous until the last two decades of the 20th century. Many a *yakuza* gangster movie hero dextrously snapped his fan open with a flick during the early 1970s. The gesture carried as much menace as the opening of a switch-blade. It was common to both samurai and *yakuza* movies; along with the carefully choreographed violence that ensues, it derives from the Kabuki theatre.

Emerging early in the 17th century, the Kabuki was the plebeian counterpart to the Noh play (see pages 102–103). Both used the fan. Of simple construction, the Noh fan was typically made of gilded paper, with a limited number of segments; it served as the prototype for the Japanese dancing (as opposed to cooling) fan. In the Kabuki, fans accompanied the aggressive posturing of the *aragoto* characters (tough guys) as it did the grace and flutter of the *onnagata* (female characters played by male actors). The choreographies of the Kabuki were later adopted by dancing geisha and are now practised by legions of women who are adepts of Japanese dancing. Still popular, *rakugo* (comic story tellers) also conjure considerable ingenuity in using a fan (open or closed) as a prop relevant to the tale.

A ceremonial fan shown in a mural in a 6th-century tomb in Fukuoka implies that the first fans to arrive in Japan were Chinese. The long-handled ceremonial version died out, but the short handled individual fan survived. Round or oval and with a rigid frame, this is the *uchiwa*. It was initially made of leather, peacock feathers or silk, the paper version coming later. A Japanese invention dating back to the 10th century, the *ōgi* (a.k.a. *sensu*) or folding paper fan was in turn adopted by the Chinese—but not until the 15th century.

During the Edo period beautiful *uchiwa*, typically decorated with woodblock prints, were common and used mainly by women. Men preferred the folding variety, always in sober colours. The average *uchiwa* nowadays has a plastic frame, is emblazoned with cartoon characters and ads, and is handy only for fanning summer barbecues.

The *sensu* remains a favourite accessory for traditional formal ladies' wear in summer, coming in as vast an array of designs and colours as the kimono. It has seen a considerable decline in recent years, but its demise is still a long way off. They are made in much of Japan, the best and most expensive coming from Kyoto. The rarity is to see an old man in some working-class neighbourhood twirling the closed fan through his fingers and, with a sudden flourish, opening it with a snap before fanning himself. In every way—cool.

Kasa

umbrellas

In summer, perhaps fortunately, Japan usually has a good rainstorm every few days to clear the intolerably muggy air. From early autumn, you can expect typhoons—the storms that can bring disaster with them in the form of flooding and landslides. Meanwhile, a fifth season occurs everywhere except Okinawa and Hokkaido for a month in early summer. This is *tsuyu* and, if you haven't already guessed, it's the rainy season.

Small wonder then that the Japanese seem to have a long and creative relationship with the umbrella or *kasa*. Umbrella racks stand behind the entrances of all public buildings; suburban railroad lost-property offices accumulate colossal collections of them. Station shopping malls always yield a number of umbrella shops stocking an amazing array of colours and styles. There are folding umbrellas, push-button umbrellas, umbrellas straight or curved-handled and disposable plastic ones. The one umbrella they won't have, however, is what is now called *wagasa* (Japanese umbrella) in contradistinction to the generic word *kasa*. Unlike the modern variety, the *wagasa* is the object of a long-standing love affair. Made of oiled paper stretched over a bamboo frame with the ribs often lacquered on the outside, its origin probably lies in the Chinese

ceremonial paper umbrellas imported sometime in the 5th century. The current *wagasa* became widespread during the Edo period (1603–1868); on the eve of the 20th century, there were still over a million of them produced from workshops all over the country. First called *kōmorigasa* (bat umbrella) because it resembled one, the black, metal framed Western umbrella gained ground fast.

Considered a thing of beauty from the outset, the *wagasa* was—and remains—a favoured traditional design motif used to decorate lacquerware, ceramics and textiles. It features prominently in countless woodblock prints (see pages 22–23). Andō Hiroshige's (1797–1858) several "Sudden Rain" themes see them in action, protagonists dashing with them through the downpour alongside others in straw raincoats or conical hats. Other prints show them as parasols for, like the conical hat, the *kasa* was also used for sheltering from the sun.

Usually comprising around 50 hand-cut ribs of select bamboo and an intricate assembly joined with a tracery of cotton string, their manufacture is a matter of consummate craftsmanship involving up to 100 steps. *Janome* (snake-eye) is the kind decorated with a thick white ring suggesting a bullseye

and usually used by women. The man's is plain and sometimes slightly larger. The *wagasa* is used in traditional Japanese dancing and in the Kabuki theatre. Variants include large red varieties for religious functions and tea ceremonies outdoors. Some of the more expensive traditional inns still lend guests the *bangasa* (number-umbrella), which bears the room number and/or *kanji* characters of the establishment's name. Produced only in a few centres today, notably in Kyoto and Gifu, genuine *wagasa* (as opposed to varieties made elsewhere in East Asia) are becoming increasingly expensive—and ominously rare.

Eating, Drinking and Entertainment

The Japanese have never been more hedonistic than from the latter half of the 20th century. There are 80,000 restaurants in Tokyo alone. Never mind the diversity, the European cuisine, the hamburger, the pizza and the 130-year-long invasion of knife and fork. The cultural core of gourmandising remains rice, held sacred for nearly two millennia. Beer is statistically the most popular alcoholic beverage, but everyone still drinks sake.

With such a multiplicity of modern audio-visual alternatives, few Japanese would have time for the entertainment that was. Yet from card games to classical theatre forms, much survives. The instrumental accompaniment to the Shintō festival has been unchanged for centuries, and ceremonial music remains much as when it came from China some 1,300 years ago. Japan's cultural evolution is often compared to the layers of an onion; things new merely come to grow over a sempiternal core.

O-hashi

お箸
chopsticks

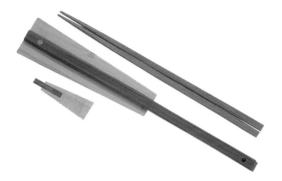

Long term foreign residents agree that one of the most infuriating things in Japan is the incredulous gushing of: "Oh, you can use chopsticks!!" Of course, most of us knew how to use chopsticks long before setting foot in Japan. Along with becoming a Pachinko pinball virtuoso or speaking fluent Japanese, however, using chopsticks is like breaking a commandment—one of the Things That Foreigners Do Not Do!

Chopsticks have probably been used in Japan for 2,000 years—ever since the Chinese and/or Koreans first set foot there. Sized midway between the larger Chinese version and the thin, tapering (and now usually metal) Korean variety, Japanese chopsticks come in a variety of forms, and are called *hashi*. Long, thick wooden ones are used for cooking; long metal ones are used like tongs for fishing things from the embers. Usually made of wood, the ordinary eating *hashi* come in different shapes and sizes too. They can be attractively decorated, notably with lacquer. Many households keep *hashi* in individual boxes for each family member. The most beautiful are reserved for special occasions like New Year celebrations.

Called *waribashi* (breaking chopsticks) and contained in paper wrappers, those used in restaurants consist of a strip of wood with a longitudinal central groove sufficiently deep for it to be broken into two halves. The best are sometimes joined only at the top and the sticks have been rounded, tapered and smoothed. The use of *waribashi* is becoming increasingly controversial: the timber used is imported mainly from Southeast Asian countries in which reforestation and conservation are low priorities, though some also come from the USA, where a Minnesota firm makes seven million *waribashi* a day. According to an estimate during the late 1980s, the Japanese use and throw away 11,000 million *waribashi* every day.

Although they would make a viable alternative, plastic chopsticks are not popular, except for small children. Being difficult to break and unchewable, they make good learning tools. Politeness is paramount to the Japanese, so it comes as no surprise that there is some elaborate etiquette regarding the use of chopsticks.

Many types of food are served in individual portions but, as in most of Asia, many dishes in Japan are traditionally placed on the table for communal use. It is important to know how each morsel is to be conveyed from dish to individual plate or rice-bowl, and into the mouth. Most of the misdemeanours involving *hashi* have names. *Namidabashi* (crying chopsticks) means allowing food or sauces to drip off your chopsticks onto the table; *tatakibashi* (hitting chopsticks) is the crime committed by the would-be after-dinner speaker tapping his chopsticks against the tableware to draw attention. Additionally, one must never wave chopsticks over the dishes and dither before homing in on one, spear pieces of food with them, or close one's mouth around them or suck them—at least not if anyone's looking. Similarly, never stick chopsticks upright in a bowl of rice (this is said to be unlucky as it evokes images of incense sticks standing in a joss bowl at a funeral) and chopsticks should always be placed on the *hashi-oki* (chopstick rest) when finished.

Japanese friends concurred about such classic no-nos in this particular social minefield, but there tend to be regional variants too. It was then that I sought counsel from the Internet. At last I discovered 'Thirteen Forbidden Behaviours with Chopsticks', but, sadly, the site was no longer extant.

Nihon-shu

日本酒
sake paraphernalia

*"This sacred sake
Is not my sacred sake,
'Tis sacred sake brewed
By Ono-mono-nushi of Yamato,
How long ago,
How long ago!"*

By the time this verse came to be written in the 8th century, sake or Japanese rice wine had manifestly been around for quite some time. The passage comes from the Kojiki, a book of records melding history with the myths at the core of the Shintō religion. In the real world meanwhile, sake came to Japan with the cultivation of rice, which is thought to have been introduced via Korea sometime around the 3rd century BC.

When fermented, rice produces a cloudy brew still characteristic of an unrefined (though nowadays commercially produced) farmhouse sake called *doburoku* (a.k.a. *nigorizake*). The similarity between this and *makali*, its Korean equivalent, would seem to speak volumes for their common origin; consumed cool, in both cases the brew presents a refreshing, slightly sour taste and would be perfect for summer but for the fact that it goes on fermenting after bottling; as the mercury rises in July, bottles have been known to explode!

Reflecting an agricultural context, the Shintō religion celebrates crop cycles and fertility, so that rice—the great Japanese staple—is held as sacred. As a by-product of rice, sake is considered sacred too. Shintō festivals are pretty bibulous affairs, and as major festivals draw near, great barrages of colourful sake

barrels pile up outside the shrines. Some are reserved for ceremonies and offerings to the gods, though the priests save the divinities the trouble of imbibing by drinking it themselves. Other barrels will be opened and consumed by celebrants during the course of the festival.

Made from rice, water and a yeast called *kōji*, sake is produced wherever rice is grown, but cooler areas with the purest spring water are likely to be best. Calling for high grade, specially polished rice, fine sake demands all the care and expertise equivalent to making vintage wine, the brewing process actually taking longer. Unlike wine, which improves with age, however, sake should be consumed within about a year from manufacture.

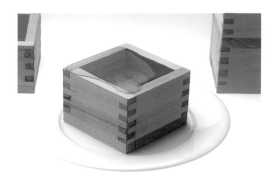

Since the late 19th century Japan has come to manufacture and import drinks of other kinds, notably beer and whisky. As a result, the word sake has been turned into a generic term for alcoholic beverages. What the rest of the world still calls sake is now known in Japan as *Nihon-shu* (Japanese alcoholic drink).

As clear as water with a smooth flavour faintly akin to sherry, *Nihon-shu* runs a gamut from *amakuchi* (sweet) to *karakuchi* (dry) with a great many categories and qualities in between. Many brands brew in three qualitative categories: *tokkyū* (special grade), *ikkyū* (first grade) and the most common *nikkyū* (second grade). The finest sake is *junmaishu* (pure rice wine). The type produced in factories adding sugar to boost the alcohol content starts with *seishu* and goes way down to the moonshine sold in vending machines. Good sake drinks easily, almost belying an alcohol content averaging between 14 to 18 percent. The hangover is notoriously dire, which has a lot to do with why modern Japan's most popular beverage is beer.

In medieval times farmers cultivated rice for their feudal lords but were forbidden to consume it, as it was considered a fermented beverage. As this relaxed during the Edo period

(1603–1868), sake consumption increased substantially. It was then that artisans and potters turned their attention more to sake drinking paraphernalia, with delightful results. Often beautifully fashioned, decorated and painted, the *tokkuri* (flasks) and little *o-choko* (sake cups) have become highly collectible—and sometimes extremely dear. *Tokkuri* come in a variety of sizes, ranging from the large earthenware flasks that sake merchants used as bottles before glass came to replace them during the 19th century, to very small containers usually destined for heated sake.

Having witnessed sake consumed warm (*atsukan*) and poured out of the heated *tokkuri* into the cups, many foreigners are convinced that this must be the only way to drink it. Not so. Sake is best drunk cold, in a glass. Connoisseurs would shudder at the thought of warming a fine sake, for heating impairs the taste; warm sake is fine, but sweeter, less elevated brews do the job best. The drier the brew and the better its quality, the more criminal the act of heating it becomes.

Cold sake is always drunk during Shintō ceremonies, especially at weddings. The bride and groom typically knock in the top of the barrel with a wooden hammer, and ladle the brew into small open-topped containers

called *masu*—one for each guest. Square and made of cedar wood, the *masu* used to be a taverner's measure but has gradually slipped into general use. The optional custom of sprinkling salt (believed to be a purifying element) around the rim may have a ritual origin, for it certainly does nothing to improve the taste. Drunkenness has never been a sin in Japan, but there is always the old cautionary proverb: "Drink your sake, but don't let it drink you."

Hyōtan

瓢箪
gourds

The Japanese seem to have a fixation on *hyōtan* (gourds). Popular as a design motif and represented singularly or severally and in various configurations, gourds adorn lacquerware and textiles; their shape is evoked in ceramic sake flasks and in silhouette as cut-outs in furniture. There are even the occasional gourd-shaped windows set in the walls of traditional houses, especially tea huts.

The gourd family (Cucurbitaceae) has several varieties, the *hyōtan* or white-flowered gourd (*Lagenaria siceraria*), which first came from Southeast Asia, being the most common in Japan. They can be very large—1 m (3 ft) long with a diameter of 50 cm (20 in). The plant is also very aptly known in English as the bottle gourd. Travellers and soldiers once used *hyōtan* as bottles for water or sake; in those days gourds counted among the *sagemono* (hanging things) dangling from their *obi* sash (see pages 58–61). In fact, before the *netsuke* was invented to toggle *sagemono* to the same, a small *hyōtan* would be used instead.

The plant is grown on a trellis, which mainly results in fruit of uniform shape, like a pear with a narrow waist. Nonetheless, since crooked, twisted, elongated and/or gnarled gourds were often more appreciated for the sheer variety of their forms, they were some-

times assisted to produce more extravagant shapes. Once dried out, the plant acquires a deep reddish-brown patina, enhanced with polishing and sometimes with lacquer. *Hyōtan* were used to make many objects, particularly bowls, scoops and spoons, though the bottle was by far the most common and popular. The practical uses of *hyōtan* have now declined, but they remain popular decorative objects and are still widely grown.

In Ibaraki prefecture near Hitachi, there is even a *hyōtan* museum, with thousands of exhibits of *hyōtan* and their many practical and decorative applications spanning from the Kamakura period (1185–1331) to the present day. Some of these items show *hyōtan* as design motifs in military hardware; the gourd

has martial associations. The shogun Toyotomi Hideyoshi (1536–1598) is said to have won a significant early victory while using a large golden *hyōtan* at the top of a pole as an ensign. Ever since, each time he won another battle, he affixed another smaller gourd beneath it.

Hyōtan are celebrated in festivals. One in Miyanoshita, near Hakone, commemorates a meeting between Hideyoshi and his two greatest generals, Tokugawa Ieyasu and Date Masamune prior to their victory at the Battle of Odawara of 1589. A *hyōtan* festival in a village in Oita prefecture, Kyushu, finds a man carousing along before the throng dressed in bright red as Hyōtan-Sama (gourd-deity).

Topped with a very tall gourd as a hat, he wears bales of straw on his feet and an out-size gourd below his waist of a fairly obvious phallic persuasion. The gourd contains sake—drinking it was believed to ward off disease and misfortune through the year.

The gourd is also the inspiration for many Japanese proverbs; examples include: '*hyōtan de namazu o osaeru*' (like trying to catch a catfish with a gourd): wasting time trying to achieve something impossible; '*hyōtan kara kouma*' (a foal emerges from a gourd): said when truth is stranger than fiction; and '*hyōtan ni tsurigane*' (comparing a gourd with a temple bell): comparing chalk and cheese.

Yōji-ire

楊枝入れ
toothpick holders

Provided it remains hidden behind the hands, picking teeth is permissible in Europe, and in most restaurants there is a toothpick holder on the table. This is equally true in Japan, but a toothpick lodged conspicuously between the teeth is a hallmark for tough-guys and *yakuza* punks. In Japan, moreover, the toothpick holder is no timid little thing hiding on the table between salt and pepper pots. It is an anarchical flight of fancy, and exempt from the obligation of matching or offseting the rest of the tableware.

Toothpick holders are made of wood, clay or metal. Along with fanciful shapes animal, vegetable and mineral, they may represent lucky deities or *bakemono* (changed things)—a word meaning both ghosts and goblins. A representation of anything ghostly would be inappropriate at table, but goblins, which no one any longer believes in, are fair game. A popular example is the *kappa*, a little chap with a flat head and webbed feet. Reported to inhabit bodies of fresh water and not as cute as he looks, the *kappa* is said to be partial to sucking the entrails from unwary swimmers. He has a dip on his flat head containing water; if it's empty he's harmless. The trick is to bow politely to him, so that he must return the compliment, spilling the water in the process.

My own weird tale of a toothpick holder actually concerns a fan, which bore a wood-block print of a bat in flight. The bat is a lucky animal in Japan and China. I was staying with my in-laws in Aichi prefecture and we were about to attend the town's annual summer fireworks spectacular. Everyone would wear *yukata* (see page 55); I was made a present of one, and my fan complemented my ensemble. Unfortunately, I put it down, and five minutes later it was gone. Later in the evening I related this uncharacteristic tale of a thing lost and not returned at the home of a family friend.

"Japanese people never do that," asserted my friend's mother. I politely countered that it could happen anywhere, but this only earned looks from my wife fit to kill. "Please accept this instead," she said, presenting me with a white porcelain toothpick holder with a vague blue decoration on the side, "It also has a picture of a bat on it."

"Oh it's lovely," I tried to enthuse, "But, er, isn't it a fish?' This was not the right thing to say at all; I should never have mentioned the loss of a mere trifle anyway. We still have the toothpick holder at home in London and, as a testimony to a disastrous faux-pas, the bat-fish swimming or flying on the side will haunt me for the rest of my days.

Tetsubin

鉄瓶
iron kettles

Few words have been devoted to the humble tea kettle in English. Entire volumes, on the other hand, have been written about the Japanese cast iron kettle. In all probability, this is because tea-drinking Europe lavished great artistic skills on the teapot and almost none to the kettle, whereas, in most instances, the Japanese had things the other way around.

Calling for exceptional artisanal skill, *tetsubin* are made using a *cire perdu* method. First the body, typically rotund or cylindrical, is shaped in lightweight wood and/or resin. Then intricate designs, including abstract patterns, friezes, plants and flowers, animals and birds are sculpted in wax and resin over the top. The model is then filled inside and coated outside with a kind of mud made of sand as fine as powder, which is packed tight by applying consecutive layers. Now a shapeless mass with holes left at strategic intervals to pour the molten metal, it is then placed in a kiln. When the liquid iron is poured, the wax and wood of the model burn away, leaving details of exquisite delicacy and sharpness. The lids and handles are often made of bronze. *Tetsubin* makers enter their craft on a hereditary basis and some extant today have been officially bestowed the title of 'Living National Treasure'.

The other special attribute of the *tetsubin* is its rather contentious connection to the tea ceremony. This is perhaps best illustrated by trying to shed light on some of the ideas expressed by Okakura Kakuzō (1862–1913). While Curator of Oriental Antiquities at the Boston Museum, Okakura famously wrote his beautiful *The Book of Tea*, both an essay on teaism and elegy on the passing of Japanese classical culture. "Like art," he wrote, "Tea has its periods and schools. Its evolution may be roughly divided into three main stages: the Boiled Tea, the Whipped Tea, and the Steeped Tea. We moderns belong to the last school."

In actual fact, other than the "we", the moderns were very much of the Whipped Tea persuasion. As a scholar and literatus, Tenjin identified with the great Tea Masters and the currents of teaism during the Edo period (1603–1868). As the tea ceremony increasingly became the preserve of ostentatious aristocrats, so the genuine teaists discreetly sought to isolate themselves from its conventional form.

By the 1640s, the expensive powdered *matcha* whisked in a bowl at the tea ceremony now had a rival in *sencha* (green tea), first imported from China but grown in Japan by the 18th century. Being overwhelmingly Chinese, however, tea-making equipment

was still expensive—until someone came up with the *tetsubin*. Preferring the steeped green tea that was being increasingly drunk anytime in ordinary households, the literati no doubt liked to boil their water in a *tetsubin*.

Substituting the subtle aesthetic mind games played by the teaist literati with hollow ceremonial, the modern followers of Sa-dō prefer *matcha*. They use the *tetsubin* only in two instances. One, as an accessory for preparing *kaiseki ryōri*, a highly refined form of cuisine served before the ceremony. Two, water is boiled in a *tetsubin* when a budding Tea Master conducts his first ceremony. Otherwise, they boil their tea not in a kettle, but in a cast iron pot. Okakura's outlook is not for them.

Karuta

かるた
card games

The word *karuta* covers a number of card games in Japan, and derives from the Latin and European word 'carta'. Indeed, card games were introduced into Japan by the Portuguese in the 16th century. Whatever the games they introduced, they were soon replaced with purely Japanese ones—using cards bearing Japanese imagery.

The Japanese have always imported things and adapted them later, but the reasons underlying the Japanization of *karuta* seem to have been prompted by necessity rather than choice. Like many things pleasing the populace, cards soon fell foul of the shogunate. Having conceded licensed quarters as a necessary evil to house things of which they disapproved (theatres, taverns, teahouses, brothels), the shogunate drew the line at gambling. But they looked away from violations of the ostensible laws governing cards, by banning specifically Portuguese gambling games; the new games invented to replace them could be played with impunity.

Although there are variants, *karuta* still comes essentially in three main forms, inspired mainly from the *kai-awase* (shell-matching) game played since Heian times (794–1185).

This comprised scores of clam shells gorgeously painted and gilded on the inside; half of them bore a picture and the other half a text, or both halves presented complementary images. Either way, the object was to match together two shells making up a whole.

Karuta adopted both the *kai-awase* formula and aesthetics. One game was *hyakunin-isshu* (100 poets and poems), based on an early 13th-century poetry compilation. One player randomly selects a card from the pack of 100 poet's cards and reads it out, minus the last few syllables. The winner is the one finding the missing words, which will be on one of the 100 corresponding cards scattered on the tatami matting. Another variant is *irohagaruta* ('syllabilary' *karuta*) played with two sets of 48 cards, similarly according to the matching of pictures and a text. The other game is *hanafuda* (flower cards) (pictured here), the one thought to be closest to the Portuguese original. Consisting of 48 cards, *hanafuda* finds four sets of 12 cards each devoted to a particular month and flower (for example February, Plum; June, Peony). This too relies on matching, but the structure of the game is comparable to Poker, so it isn't surprising that *hanafuda* has always been prized by serious gamblers.

Igo

囲碁
go games

Counting millions of adepts all over the world, not to mention associations in the USA and both a European and International Go Federation, the game of *igo* (the correct name for *go*) can now even be played live on-line.

So how is it played? With two players, one with 181 black stones and the other with 180 white ones. Black always begins. The game is played on a board called a *goban*, which is properly composed of 19 by 19 squares or 361 intersections, though boards squared to a ratio of 13 or 9 are not unusual. The game progresses with the placing of a stone on an empty spot where the lines on the board intersect; if a stone or group of stones is surrounded by those of the opponent, it is captured and removed from the board. Players' scores are calculated according to the number of points scored for walling up the opponent's stones, minus the number of stones lost. The calculations are further complicated by points scored for various other moves and considerations; *igo* rivals even chess for skill and strategy.

Called *weiqi* in Chinese, the game of *igo* is thought to have originated in China as much as 4,000 years ago. Players' skills are measured according to a *dan* system like martial arts, ranging from one to seven in both amateur and professional categories. The perfect game, however, has never been won. Mathematicians have calculated that since the black starts, it must ultimately win—but no one has ever managed to prove it on the board. Efforts to devise a computer program for discovering the perfect game have so far yielded no conclusive results.

Japanese *igo* used to differ slightly from variants in other countries. Based on a real tournament in 1938, the writer Yasunari Kawabata's (1899–1972) famous novel *The Master of Go* develops the real game between a dying grand master and a younger champion into an allegory for a changing Japan. The contest lasted six months—not unusual for championship games of *igo* at the time. With increasing internationalization, however, the rules have tightened and the allotted time grown shorter.

Kawabata had it that the Master's final match was plagued by modern rationalism, "to which fussy rules are everything, from which all the grace and elegance of Go as art had disappeared, which quite dispensed with respect for elders and attached no importance to mutual respect as human beings. From the way of Go the beauty of Japan and the Orient had fled."

Nohmen

能面
noh masks

Having killed the young general Atsumori in battle, Kumagai is so filled with remorse that he becomes a monk. On his way to pray at Atsumori's grave years later, a grass-cutter he encounters transpires to be Atsumori's ghost. Having re-enacted his own death, the forgiving spirit asks the grieving priest to pray for him—and disappears. Despite the simplicity of the plot, *Atsumori* lasts some two hours.

It's an archetypical Noh mask drama from a surviving repertoire of some 250, of which less than half are still performed. Borrowing from ancient shrine dances, court dances and rustic festival performances, Noh is derived above all from *sarugaku* (monkey music), a long-extinct predecessor. During the 14th century in Kyoto, Kan'ami Kyotsugu refined these ingredients into Noh (literally meaning 'skill'), which was particularly admired by the shogun Ashikaga Yoshimitsu. Becoming Yoshimitsu's protegé, Kan'ami's even more talented son Zeami Motokiyo (1363–1444) honed the art into its definitive form and wrote many of the Noh drama's finest plays.

Evolving under shogunate patronage, Noh became an exclusive samurai preserve; in the Tokugawa period (1603–1868), commoners were forbidden to see it. Performed by male actors wearing masks, Noh dramas fall into

five categories, the plays being about gods, warriors (like *Atsumori*), women, insanity and revenge or demons. A play begins with the *waki* (secondary character) establishing the context involving the *shite* (main character), who enters accompanied by an attendant. The next section describes actions preceding the play. After this comes the *kyōgen*, or comic interlude, which, often unrelated to the plot, is a theatre form in itself. Lastly, the climactic final movement typically culminates as the main character reveals himself to be a ghost or demon. For instance, in *Tsuchigumo*, one of the most popular plays, a priest returns in a leering demon mask as the spider he really is, sending long strands of paper 'web' streaming over the stage as a finale.

Performed against a painted backdrop of a pine tree and with minimal props, the Noh features lavish silk brocade costumes and exquisitely fashioned wooden masks. The masks are designed and crafted with great subtlety; they can appear to transform very dramatically simply from the alterations of light and shadow as the actors move their heads. The pace is hypnotically slow, but the movement—learned, like martial arts, according to principles rooted in Zen—delivers great dramatic power. Noh is not so much drama as

a form of opera. The words are chanted to a backing of flute and drums; the appeal lies also in rhythm and musicality.

Becoming a Noh actor is generally a hereditary privilege. There are five main schools of Noh—the Kanze, Kita, Hōshō, Konparu and Kongō—as well as the equally old Umewaka, still fighting for recognition as an independent sixth. To most modern audiences, the ancient courtly language of the Noh is incomprehensible; spectators often follow the action as they read the translation in their programmes.

Modern Noh plays have been written by, among others, the author Mishima Yukio, and the minimalist beauty of the form continues to exert considerable influence on modern Japanese theatre.

Wagakki

和楽器

musical instruments

Ethnocentrism was considered almost a *sine qua non* for encounters of the cultural kind among late 19th-century western travellers to the Far East. Nowhere is this more apparent than in their impressions of Japanese music.

"But oh!" narrow-mindedly lamented one in 1905, "the music itself to us foreigners was too appalling for words. Strident was not the word for it, it was perfectly ear-piercing. And if one could attempt to fairly describe it, the combination of the sounds produced by a bagpipe at close quarters out of tune, the squealing of a dying pig, the rumbling of a tumbrel and the wail of a lost soul might partially do so."

Given the reference to the bagpipe, there can be little doubt that he was referring to the *gagaku* orchestra, which has accompanied all Imperial and religious ceremonies and rituals for well over 1,000 years. Of distant Indian origin, the instruments it comprises came into Japan from China during the T'ang dynasty. These were notably the *biwa* (a lute) (see right and above), the *koto* (a 13-stringed zither), various flutes and percussion instruments including the *tsuzumi* shoulder drum and the large, upright *da-daiko* drum. Rather than ear-piercing, *gagaku* music is very grand and sedate. It owes its particular sound quality

to the *shō*, a kind of mouth organ with vertical pipes (a distant ancestor of the western pipe organ), variants of which exist in China and South East Asia. Popular for court entertainments in pre-medieval Japan, some *gagaku* instruments (but not the *shō*) became widely adopted in less formal contexts from the 10th century. They have been widely used in Japanese traditional music ever since.

Buddhist chanting strongly influenced singing in Japan, where itinerant monks often gathered alms by singing epic poems to a *biwa* accompaniment. Adopted in secular contexts, notably in *naga-uta* (long songs) from the 13th century, and in the Noh theatre from the late 1400s, their style provided the basis of the *jōruri* (dramatic ballad) singing in the Kabuki theatre in the 17th century. Such songs were also performed by geisha, as well as by blind minstrels, who continued to have an official monopoly on singing epic poems until 1871. Plangent and heavily stylised, the classic technique is an acquired taste to many modern Japanese used to Western harmony. In 1889, Pierre Loti decried the singing of a "quite young, fairly pretty" geisha who had "a voice that might have belonged to an aged frog, a ventriloquist's voice, coming from whence it would be impossible to say."

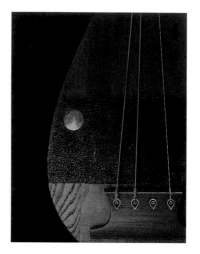

Whatever he thought, however, classical Japanese singing still finds audiences and performers today.

Now considered the most Japanese of instruments, the *shamisen* gradually eclipsed the *biwa* during the Edo period. First introduced from China via Okinawa, it is a three-stringed lute similar to a banjo, with a long, thin neck and a small round sound box covered in snake (Okinawa) or animal skin (mainland Japan). Adopted in the Kabuki theatre, it soon became the instrument of choice for geisha, blind minstrels and for folk music in general. Today lively *shamisen* folk traditions thrive in Tsugaru, in Tohoku and down in Okinawa. Elsewhere, like too many manifestations of Japanese culture, *shamisen* playing has become a form of occupational therapy for housewives.

Following the abandonment of a shorter counterpart some 500 years earlier, the *shakuhachi*, a rim-blown bamboo flute about 45 cm (18 in) long (see above), re-emerged during the Edo period. Presenting the player with great scope for expression, its unique tone quality make it a popular instrument in a broad range of musical contexts today, including contemporary music and jazz.

Ningyō Jōruri

人形浄瑠璃
marionette theatre

In the Bunraku, it takes three men to operate a single puppet and they manipulate it on the stage. It sounds an unwieldly formula for captivating an audience, but the movement of the marionettes is so uncannily lifelike that the puppeteers, soon forgotten, seem to vanish. Therein lies the magic of *ningyō jōruri*, the Japanese puppet play, which the word Bunraku has come to signify. This goes back to the Bunraku-za, a theatre a canny puppeteer named Uemura Bunrakuken opened in Osaka in 1872. Still based in Osaka, the Bunraku is Japanese marionette theatre at its most refined, but its roots go back much further.

Bunrakuken himself came from Awajima island in Osaka Bay. This is the home of the *kugutsu-mawashi*, itinerant entertainers who played at village festivals, carrying glove-puppets in a box strapped around their necks. Known in Japan since the 8th century, such puppeteering is of Chinese origin. It is believed to have come from Korea, with many of the first protagonists having settled on Awajima island. Puppeteering remained comparatively primitive for centuries, despite erstwhile developments in Japanese drama and music.

Chanted poems and epic ballads had been popular since the 12th century but, following the introduction of the *shamisen* (see pages

104–105) in the early 16th century, the style was gradually transformed into a more dramatized form of sung story-telling. So popular was one tale, about a tragic love affair between the (fictional) princess Jōruri and (historical) warrior Yoshitsune, that the style of singing with *shamisen* accompaniment became known as *jōruri* for all time.

At the end of the 16th century, puppet plays in Kyoto and Osaka began featuring *jōruri* narration, an idea soon adopted in the Kabuki theatre. These puppet plays were known as *ningyō* (doll) *jōruri*. During the early 17th century in Edo (now Tokyo), the *jōruri* singer Satsuma Jōun brought puppet drama to new heights with plays about the swordsman Kimpira, whose swagger is said to have inspired the *aragoto* (tough-guy) characters in the Kabuki theatre. The plays were extremely violent; the puppets were often damaged. Overcome with excitement, the narrating Jōun is said to have participated in the carnage, often reaching out to seize one of the puppets and smashing its wooden head to bits!

1685 saw the opening of a new theatre Takemoto-za in Osaka, which teamed noted puppet master and celebrated *jōruri* singer Takemoto Gidayu with dramatist Chikamatsu

Monzaemon (1653–1725). Often described as a Japanese Shakespeare, Chikamatsu covered a large range of subject matter. About the tragedies that haunted the pleasure quarters, notably illicit love affairs culminating in double suicides, his most famous plays introduced social realism. Though it is said he preferred puppets (less troublesome than capricious Kabuki actors), Chikamatsu wrote, like most erstwhile dramatists, both for Kabuki and *ningyō jōruri*; the two were interchangeable.

From 1734 the puppets had grown large enough to require three manipulators. The leader is the *omo-zukai*, responsible for the head and right arm. Looking after the left arm, the *hidari-zukai* deals with any props such as fans, swords, and so on, the puppet may pick up. The *ashi-zukai* looks after the feet. Having no legs, female puppets require a special technique involving a hoop beneath the skirt and bunched fists to suggest movement in the knees. Bunraku comands commensurate skill; the puppeteers, like the musicians and narrators, generally adopt the profession on a hereditary basis.

Meanwhile, some of Japan's more rustic puppet forms still exist, notably on Shikoku island, in Iida City in Nagano prefecture and on Awajima island, which is where it all started.

Karakuri

からくり
mechanical toys

Coming in a variety of shapes and sizes from elaborate puppets to mechanical toys, *karakuri* first appeared during the 18th century. The archetype would be the tea-boy shown to me by Tamaya Shobei VIII, whose family has been making *karakuri* for well over 200 years. Standing about 50 cm (20 in) high, the doll represented a boy in a brocade kimono, proudly holding a wooden coaster out in front of him, bearing a cup of green tea. Beginning to whirr, he trundled across the tatami on the workshop floor with occasional nods of an immaculately crafted wooden head, then came to a stop before me. Once I had emptied the cup and replaced it on the tray, the doll turned around and went back to its starting point.

At their workshop-home in Nagoya, the Tamayas produce a number of ingenious wooden *karakuri* in addition to these tea carriers. Natives of Chubu, central Japan, *karakuri* are versed in a variety of skills. Attired in gorgeous silks and brocades and coming into their own as the star attractions during festivals in Takayama and Nagoya, they perform feats with astounding precision. Atop ornate carnival floats towering above the gaping throng, they variously climb ladders, turn somersaults, swing from trapezes and even deftly execute calligraphy with a brush.

Virtually the only time to see *karakuri* in action is during the festivals; when not gathering dust in museums, the majority are hidden away in Shintō shrines and regarded as sacred. The origin of the *karakuri*, however, is more profane. They appeared first in the Osaka pleasure quarters in the early 18th century, and were popular items in tea-houses and sideshows. Most performed acrobatic stunts but some were ribald, one appearing to fill himself up with sake and urinate. There were even moving puppet tableaux with details such as mechanical fish leaping from ponds.

Small wonder that Japanese electronics and automation professionals hail the *karakuri* as the ancestor of the Japanese robot. The link between them and high-tech is exemplified by Hisashige Tanaka, a 19th-century master clockmaker who also made *karakuri*, including a tea-carrier. Turning to manufacturing in the 1860s, he founded a company now known by the name of Toshiba.

Like the automatons in Europe, the *karakuri* were made during the 18th century mostly by clockmakers. In those days, however, Japanese technology lagged far behind; there was nothing to compare with the elaborate metal European equivalents capable of dancing or playing real musical instruments.

Nonetheless, both despite and because of their limitations, the *karakuri* were works of genius. The only metal parts were governors; the wheels, gears and ratchets driving them were made of wood and they were assembled only with wooden pegs. Winding springs were made of baleen, the whalebone used to make corsets in Victorian times. The delicate balance needed to activate stunts was achieved using sliding blobs of mercury or trickling sand.

A workshop like the Tamaya produces about 10 *karakuri* per year. Not a lot, but they take months to make. *Karakuri* command prices running into tens of thousands of dollars, so most are commissioned by big corporations or official groups for public display. The city of Nagoya, for instance, recently presented a Tamaya tea-boy to Los Angeles, its sister city. That said, there are plenty of much more modest *karakuri* toys in Japan, but, as antiques, they never come cheap.

Custom and Religion

Almost everyone in Japan embraces two religions: Buddhism and Shintō. Coming to Japan in the 6th century, the former is a newcomer compared to the latter, an animist farmer's religion rooted in prehistory. In today's distinctly agnostic Japan, both survive as matters of form and ceremony—considerations more important than faith in Japanese society.

Traditional Japanese culture owes almost everything to Buddhism—ink painting, poetry, flower arrangement, the tea ceremony, gardens, incense and, if you went back far enough, numeracy and literacy. Shintō advocates that there are spirits in everything under and including the sun. Combined or separate, both religions left a lasting legacy of superstition—tales and legends, talismans and lucky cat statuettes, as well as customs, festivals and pastimes which still go to the heart of life in Japan.

Shimenawa

注連縄
sacred ropes

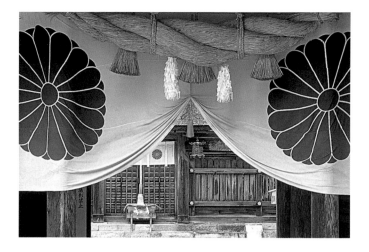

A thick rope made of plaited rice-straw, the *shimenawa* is generally suspended over the lintel or across the entrance of Shintō shrines. Demarcating the frontier between earth and the realm of the gods, it also serves to exclude evil spirits—an asset utilized each Japanese New Year, when home decorations include a *shimenawa* hanging on or near the front door. The size of the shrine reflects the size of the *shimenawa*. At Izumo *taisha*, Japan's second most sacred shrine, the colossal *shimenawa* hanging over the lintel dwarfs the devotees passing below. But even the tiniest hamlet boasts a Shintō shrine and many homes contain a *kamidana* (god-shelf)—often a model of a shrine complete with its own miniature *shimenawa*.

Meaning 'the Way of the Gods', Shintō is an animist folk religion with its origins lost in prehistory. The deities are *kami*, the gods once believed to inhabit all things under and including the sun. There are many thousands of Shintō shrines; thought to have existed for some 1700 years, the most sacred is at Ise, and the grand shrine at Izumo, which may even predate it, is a close second. The *shimenawa* may well be as old as the religion itself. The same goes for Sumo wrestling: amateur bouts are sometimes held at local Shintō shrines. It is

no coincidence that *yokozuna,* the name for a Sumo grand champion, means 'side rope'. Having won the decisive bout, the national grand champion is presented with just such a rope—a form of *shimenawa.*

Shintō ceremonies, whether inaugurating a building site or factory, for example, or simply at the shrine itself, evidence extreme antiquity. Waving branches of leaves towards cardinal points to ward off evil spirits, priests and *miko* (shrine maidens) employ a gestural repertoire similar to the shamans of Korea, Mongolia and China. From around the 5th century, Chinese influences gradually turned Shintō into an ancestor cult; everyone, especially emperors, would become *kami* after death. Although Buddhism was adopted from the mid 6th century, it merely coexists with Shintō. Being Shintōist is synonymous with being Japanese.

Moved by awe and reverence rather than faith or piety, Shintō preaches no scriptures; it is vague, heterogenous and its gods go undepicted. The Shintō priesthood is an hereditary post for officiating at ceremonies and serving the community by maintaining the shrine. Having their own titular gods, different communities believe in variants of the creation myths; until 1872, when it was formalized, the religion had no name.

Based on 8th-century chronicles melding myth and history, the resulting State Shintō was really a nationalist political expedient to promote emperor worship. It professed that Japan, its population and the gods were all the progeny of the female Izanami and the male Izanagi, who were also the parents of the sun goddess Amaterasu, the mother of emperor Jimmu—the first of an unbroken imperial line. Centuries later, having served to fuel warlike patriotic fanaticism, State Shintō was abolished in 1946.

Above all, Shintō is a farmer's religion. Bound to crop cycles, the emperor's ritual duties still include the ceremonial planting and harvesting of rice in the palace grounds. From convivial New Year bonfires in remote country shrines to spectacular annual festivals attended by hundreds of thousands, Shintō serves to bond the community. The gods are invoked for a safe journey, success in exams or business, the birth of a child or protection against illness.

If few believe intrinsically today, everyone likes to play safe—and perhaps it was always so. To illustrate this, when standing before the altar at Ise Jingū, the 13th-century poet-priest Saigyo owned: "I know not at all if anything deigns to be there." Nevertheless, he was moved to tears of reverence.

Ema

絵馬
votive plaques

A small rectangular wooden plaque topped with a triangle like a low roof, the *ema* looks like the gabled end of a Shintō shrine. Similar to the Roman Catholic ex-voto, it is purchased by devotees who inscribe it with prayers. The *ema* is then suspended from one of the bars on a wooden rack specially provided for the purpose in the shrine compound. The similarity with the Christian ex-voto ends abruptly with the nature of the prayers. Some are prayers of thanks, but many would be requests for things as materialistic as a successful business venture or a lottery win. It is believed the Shintō gods—especially Inari, the deity of grain and gain revered both by farmers and business people—understand these things. Shrines dedicated to Inari are dotted about with many stone statues of seated foxes (Inari's messenger or familiar); likewise the *ema* may be decorated with a picture of a fox.

The customary visit to shrines during O-shōgatsu (New Year) is a bit like taking out a comprehensive all-risk insurance policy from the gods. The shrines dedicated to Inari are among the most popular; visitors to Fushimi Inari near Kyoto, for instance, run into millions per annum. In addition to the *ema*, there are many other charms and talismans on sale any time of year; examples include *o-mamori* (talismans which keep the bearer safe from misfortune) (see pages 126–127) and *o-mikuji* (random numbered fortune papers tied to a tree for luck).

Ema can be used at any time and are not confined to any special occasion. Students often buy them at shrines dedicated to Tenjin—the deified spirit of Sugawara Michizane (845–903), a great scholar and statesman who was ousted by intriguing rivals and died in exile a broken man. Tenjin shrines all over Japan swarm with students as exams draw near, when the *ema* trade is particularly brisk.

As Shintō was essentially a folk religion, its ceremonies were all connected to crop cycles. Human and vegetable fertility were often inextricably bound together, as is evidenced by the small—if fairly conspicuous—number of shrines devoted to phallicism and fertility. The shrine compound in these display symbols of male and female genitalia in stone or wood, so *ema* at such shrines are usually decorated with phallic symbols, the inscriptions on them prayers for children, or remedies for infertility, impotence, and increasingly, protection from or a cure for HIV and AIDS.

Sometimes, *ema* are also presented in Buddhist temples. There are many instances of the overlay between Shintō and Buddhism, which explains the presence of essentially Shintōist *ema* in temples—especially those predating the establishment of State Shintō in the 1870s, when the two religions were forcibly kept apart.

During the Edo period (1603–1868), *ema* took the form of much larger paintings than the little plaques so common today. The main hall of the colossal Sensoji temple in Asakusa, Tokyo, for instance, displays several. A telling proportion depict horses as, indeed, *ema* formerly always did. In the days when a horse was essential for transport, it was the most generous offering one could make to a Shintō shrine. But horses were expensive; even those who could afford them thought twice about presenting one. Instead they left a statue or a painting of a horse; the meaning of the word *ema* translates as 'horse picture'.

Hasu-no-hana

蓮の花
lotus flowers

The lotus flower is one of the most important symbols in Buddhism. Effigies of the Buddha depict him seated upon one; the Lotus Sutra is one of the most important prayers among Japanese Buddhists. There are often lotus flowers of carved wood or bronze set in vases before the Buddha on the temple altar. The flower comes in several configurations, the more stylized versions showing a striking similarity with equivalent design motifs from ancient Egypt. The religion originated in India, but such designs had been adopted in India long before the religion made its way to Japan through Tibet and China.

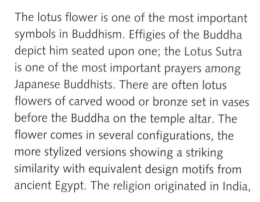

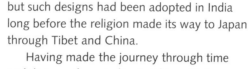

Having made the journey through time and distance from India via China, Mahayana (Great Vehicle) Buddhism was introduced to Japan by Korean emissaries in the middle of the 6th century, and decreed a state religion by Prince Shōtoku in 593. Buddhist influence increased substantially during the Nara period (710–794) and even more during the Heian era (794–1185) with the creation of the Tendai sect, which was one of the first to combine elements of Buddhism and Shintō together. Other sects popular today have origins equally old, including the Shingon, founded by Kūkai (774–835). Currently prominent, Amida (Pure Land) Buddhism appeared during the 13th century; among its offshoots are the Jōdo and Jōdo Shinshū, which also have a wide following today. Founded by Nichiren (1222–1282), Nichiren-shū has millions of followers and numerous sub-sects worldwide, including the influential modern Sōka Gakkai.

Zen Buddhism was introduced from China during the Kamakura period. It discards scrip-

tures and doctrine; enlightenment is attainable only through individual effort, *zazen* or special meditation, and abstinence. Among Zen sects, the Sōtō and Rinzai have a wide following today. Particularly favoured by the samurai, Zen had a profound and lasting influence on Japanese culture, underlying the tea ceremony, for example (see pages 134–137).

Among the traditional stores found in any Japanese neighbourhood, the *butsudan-ya* (Buddha-shelf shop) is where you would look for a representation of a lotus flower—in carved wood, gilded metal or even plastic. It also sells the *butsudan* or home Buddhist altar itself. Usually a cabinet of dark or black-lacquered wood, the *butsudan* has doors which open up onto an altar of hand-carved, gilt wood and is primarily used for the remembrance of deceased relatives. Their photographs grace the altar, along with sticks of incense, offerings and such items as the gilded temple flowers. As the overwhelming majority of Japanese practice both Shintō and Buddhism, Orthodox Japanese homes would have both a *kamidana* (god-shelf) to appease the Shintō gods and a *butsudan*.

Jizō Bosatsu

地蔵菩薩
votive statues

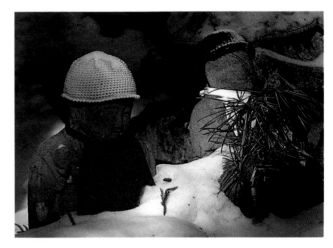

Often seen singly or in groups, both by the roadside or on temple precincts, the small stone statue of the Jizō *bosatsu* represents a patron deity for travellers and children. Wearing a monk's habit and bearing the staff of a wandering priest, it is usually a round-faced, child-like figure rarely standing more than one metre (3 ft) tall. One of the most ubiquitous—and curious—icons of Buddhism in Japan, Jizō represents the *bodhisattva* (*bosatsu*) known in India as Ksitigarbha. Legend has it that, during the era between the departure of Gautama (the historical Buddha) and Maitreya (the still-awaited Buddha of the future), the *bodhisattva* Jizō vowed to roam all six realms of existence and help to salvation every being he met.

The invocation of the *bodhisattva*'s boundless compassion is variously construed. There's Hōroku (stoneware-bowl) Jizō for headaches and neckaches, and Togenuki (splinter removal) Jizō, both in temples in Tokyo's Komagome. Standing at what was once the old Kotsukappara execution ground (now near Sanya, Tokyo's only slum), Kubikiri (head-chop) Jizō was placed there in the mid 18th century and is thought to have saved the souls of some 150,000-odd victims of the executioner's sword.

Of all the variants, the travelling saint concept may be the more ancient. Its features eroded and overgrown with lichen, it stands frequently alongside the *dōsojin* (roadside deities) which, predating Buddhism, still stand often on the confines of towns and villages. Usually represented as a male and female deity standing side by side, the *dōsojin* were sometimes nothing more than a stone, which was often unabashedly phallic. *Dōsojin* were associated with fertility worship and ancient Japanese folk religion acknowledged that fertility in humans and crops were part of the same principle and the province of the same deities. Introduced to Japan in the 6th century, Buddhism remained the exclusive province of the aristocracy. Drives to popularize it from the 8th century involved turning Shintō deities into Buddhist *bodhisattvas*; the success of the ploy partly explains why Jizō has to suffer the indignity of standing alongside phallic symbols. Indeed, the shape of the Jizō statue is itself pretty phallic; if you go behind the one near Shinobazu pond in Tokyo's Ueno park, the likeness is much too studied for coincidence.

Fertility and progeny are closely allied. The Jizō is also the patron of children but, above all, the guardian of the souls of those unborn. Unborn children are *mizuko* or 'water children',

the expression used for foetuses. Women pray that the result of their miscarriages may enter heaven, but also seek to appease the little souls of those they have had aborted by making offerings to a Jizō or buying a Jizō statuette.

Myth has it that the *mizuko* enter a kind of purgatory, a river bank in the dark realm of the dead where they spend their time stacking stones, in the belief that it will please their living parents. Every night they endure having their work destroyed by a demoness, forcing them to start again the next day. Hearing their cries, however, Jizō leads them on to the paradise on the other side.

On some temple compounds, the little grey Jizō statues number several hundredfold in seried ranks. Wearing bright red bibs, the newer ones simply placed over the faded and frayed ones underneath, they stand in a forest of coloured pinwheels, dolls and plastic wind-mills put there by anxious women. In Kyoto there is a modern Jizō temple in which effigies are stuck in glass cases—the Buddhist equivalent of the capsule hotel. Despite some recent liberalization of the birth-control pill in Japan, contraception remained illegal until near the end of the 21st century, and the abortion rate remains one of the highest in the world—as the enduring proliferation of Jizō statues indicates.

Chōchin

提灯
paper lanterns

The Western propensity for enhancing interiors with hints of orientalism never goes out of fashion. Many people in the West are fond of cladding light bulbs in lightweight, folding white paper shades based upon the Japanese lantern. Never mind that the Japanese now vastly prefer the sad grey glare of striplighting, never mind that if they have lampshades at all, most prefer them Western style. The paper lantern remains one of the most enduring icons of Japan outside the country—notwithstanding that lanterns never really were a feature of the traditional Japanese home. In the days before electricity, illumination came from candles or oil lamps, which were usually placed inside a box-shaped shade of wood and paper—a lighting appliance called *andon*. Even today, in traditional Japanese interiors, room lighting still reflects the *andon* rather than the rounded paper lantern favoured in the West and known in Japan as *chōchin*.

In any event, the proper place for a *chōchin* is outdoors, not in. In the old days they served often as street lamps, standing atop posts by the road, dangling from the eaves of little curved roofs. Every home kept a number of *chōchin*, often folded in boxes in the entrance hall; people used them to light their way out at night. Specialist stores make

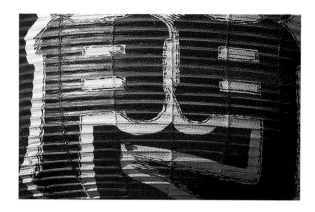

chōchin to measure. Local taverns serving snacks still announce themselves with large *aka chōchin* (red lanterns), emblazoned with characters in black; they adorn food-sellers' carts too. Lanterns covered with lettering are often used for adorning store-fronts. Although they electrified years ago, you still see strings of lanterns in shopping precincts, festooning telegraph poles and shedding lights over summer beer gardens.

When not for commercial purposes, the Japanese lantern is used mainly at festivals and funerals. At the latter, white *chōchin* adorned with the name and family crest of the deceased in black predominate. There is thus a connection between the festive lantern and death. *Chōchin* feature so prominently during Obon, the annual festival of the dead held in July, that it is celebrated as the Lantern Festival in many places. Unlike in Europe, where ghosts are believed to walk abroad in winter, the Japanese summer is the season of the dead. One of Katsushika Hokusai's most famous woodblock prints shows the terrifying face of the vengeful Oiwa, appearing in a lantern to haunt the husband who murdered her (see pages 22–23). Every summer yields a crop of horror movies and ghost plays on television and in the Kabuki theater.

One of the most famous sources of subject matter concerning *chōchin* is the story "Botandōrō", or "Peony Lantern". Based on an old Chinese tale, it was so masterfully recounted in English by Lafcadio Hearn that his version remains the definitive one to the Japanese. The tale concerns the hapless samurai youth Shinzaburō, who yearns for his lover O-Tsuyu, from whom he is estranged. Meanwhile, believing that he has forsaken her, she pines away and dies. The following year on a sultry summer night, Shinzaburō catches sight of her with her servant Oyone —the latter carrying a lantern decorated with peonies. O-Tsuyu assures him that he is mistaken, but as far as he can see, she and her servant are very much alive. A wise old priest warns Shinzaburō that this is not the case; he explains that the nocturnal visitors constantly returning to his house with the peony lantern are spirits haunting him to death. Having paid too little heed, one morning Shinzaburō is found dead, lying entwined with a skeleton whose bony hands are around his neck! With such an abundance of tales like these, small wonder the Japanese prefer to keep their lanterns outdoors.

Maneki-neko

招き猫
beckoning cats

Sitting up with one paw raised, the *maneki-neko* (beckoning cat) has recently become a familiar figure in any country possessing a Chinatown. The cat used to be confined to trading premises of all description in Japan, from shops and offices to restaurants and even 'Soapland' massage parlours. Outside Japan, you are more likely to see the *maneki-neko* in Chinese stores and restaurants than in their Japanese equivalent. A lucky charm said to boost business profits, the *maneki-neko* had gone global by the end of the 21st century, suggesting that its rising popularity among the Chinese is commensurate with Japan's economic performance during the 1980s.

Like the Manx in the UK, the majority of Japanese cats have no tails, but in the case of the *maneki-neko*, this is not visible as the cat is always sitting down. Staring straight out with bright, appealing eyes, it is usually a stylized evocation of the most common Japanese feline: Mike-chan (dear little three-colours). These colours indicate white fur with patches of black and red tabby, any combination that spawned many generations of low-pedigree mix and match. Many of today's *maneki-neko* parallel the alley cat in terms of artistry too; over-large, redolent with cartoon cuteness and garish, they are not exactly refined.

The typical *maneki-neko* is white with patches of red and black. However, there are variants, the most common being black, as well as *maneki-neko* in red, gold or silver. Usually ceramic, *maneki-neko* can also be made of papier mâché, plaster or wood. The ones with the right paw raised are for general good luck; a raised left paw specifically augurs financial gain.

The origin of the *maneki-neko* is oft-debated: some say it originated in Edo (now Tokyo) and others in Osaka or Kyoto. Such contention harks back to the days when Edo was the nation's political and military capital, and Kyoto the imperial and religious one. There is little doubt that the beckoning cat emerged during the Edo period (1603–1868); the oldest examples date back to the mid 17th century.

Although there is the odd demonic variant, the cat is generally considered a lucky animal in Japan. There are several cat temples or feline cemeteries adjoining a Buddhist temple, the most famous being Nekodera (cat temple) in Kanazawa and Ekō-in and Gōtoku-ji in Tokyo. Ekō-in has a statue commemorating a cat who once came home to his owner with a gold coin in his mouth, enabling the man, a recently bankrupted merchant, to rebuild his fortune. Most people say that the temple where the *maneki-neko* really originated was Gōtoku-ji; documents to prove it are said to go back to the 17th century.

The story behind this temple concerns the abbot of Gōtoku-ji, which was then a forlorn temple in a sorry state of repair. "If only you were a man," he lamented one stormy day to his pet cat, "you could go out and earn some money!" With that, the cat bounded out into the rain! Meanwhile, Ii Naomasa (1590–1659), the great lord of Hikone castle in Ii province, was entering Edo after a long journey along the Tokaido road with his retainers. All were soaked; along the way they saw the black cat sitting before a temple gate. As they passed, it raised his paw. Interested, Naomasa dismounted and went towards it, whereupon the cat walked a few paces and sat down again, beckoning with his paw. Following the cat, Naomasa was led to the abbot, who offered them shelter for the night. Having noted how dilapidated the temple was, Naomasa was moved by the extreme poverty of this generous priest and decided to reward him. Spending lavishly on restoration work, Naomasa turned Gōtoku-ji into his family temple. Gōtoku-ji prospers even now.

Tanuki

狸
racoon-dogs

During the 19th century, authors writing about Japan in English frequently mentioned badgers, but there are no badgers in Japan. What they meant was the *tanuki* (*Nyctereutes procyonoides*)—more accurately known as the racoon-dog. A small, nocturnal mammal with a pointed muzzle, the *tanuki* is a canid, though it suggests a racoon with its rounded ears and dark mask, not to mention short legs and stocky build. Sometimes keeping them as pets, the Japanese are specially fond of the *tanuki*, which many believe to be unique to Japan. As with so many of those 'unique' Japanese things, however, this is not the case.

The *tanuki* dates back to when Japan was joined to the mainland, before the ice age. Found in China and Siberia, this charming creature was introduced into Russia by furriers sometime in the early 20th century. Descendents of lucky escapees have spread steadily westward; the *tanuki* has been recorded in Germany and northeastern France.

The *tanuki* can cover as much as 20 km (8 miles) daily in search of food. That certainly seems a long way to go for a small omnivore, but whether that makes it specially greedy is moot. The Japanese would contend that it is. *Tanuki soba*, after all, is a hugely popular and substantial soup dish containing buckwheat noodles and a list of ingredients sufficiently varied to please a *tanuki*.

Folk belief attributes magical qualities to the *tanuki*; like the fox, it can assume human form. When not the benign messenger of the Shintō god Inari, however, the fox is seen as slightly sinister. In the old days, the mad were said to be 'possessed by fox spirits'. The *tanuki* can assume a whole gamut of other forms in addition to the human, but it only does it for laughs. There was a genuine report during the late 19th century that a mischievous *tanuki* had turned itself into an express train, but the most famous *tanuki* tale concerns a poor woodcutter who saved a *tanuki*'s life. Out of gratitude, the animal changed into a tea kettle, which the wood-cutter later sold to a priest at Morin temple. The *tanuki* wasn't at all happy with the out-come. He hated being polished, and being heated was even worse. So to the monks' amazement, just as it was put over the fire, the kettle sprouted legs and started running around. Once cornered, it changed back into a *tanuki*. One ending has it that the *tanuki* was allowed to live a lazy, unpolished and unheated life at the temple; another that he returned to the woodcutter, who made a fortune exhibiting his dancing tea-kettle.

Often found in the hallways or against the façades of restaurants and sake shops, a ceramic figure of a fat *tanuki* stands up on his hind legs with a wide-brimmed straw hat hanging down his back. A lot of people put them in their gardens, the equivalent of the western garden gnome. These are still made in Shigaraki near Kyoto, where they originated in the 18th century as a caricature of the typical profligate of the floating world. The story goes that he beats upon his bloated stomach like a drum; the same applies to his outsize scrotum, which reaches down to the ground. In one paw he holds an empty sake bottle; in the other he holds an account book —his money being wasted on wine and women. Some say that the vast scrotum is due to sexual over-indulgences but, since his penis has disappeared, another interpretation is more likely. A reminder perhaps, as Shakespeare put into the mouth of the drunken porter in Macbeth, that drink "provokes the desire, but takes away the performance!" Needless to say, 19th-century Japanologists preferred to refer to the *tanuki* as the Tea Kettle of Morin Temple.

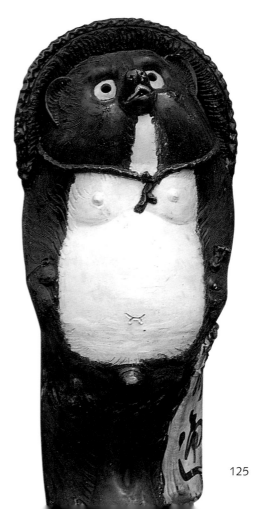

O-mamori

御守
talismans

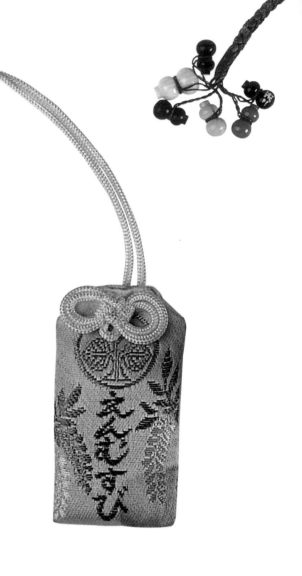

The lines of division between Shintōism and Buddhism can sometimes be pretty nebulous. With just a few interruptions, the two religions have coexisted completely; despite ostensible bans in the 1870s, there are even sects melding the two together. At first sight, the two would be wholly incompatible. Being devoted to peaceful retreats and meditation when it isn't dealing with funerals, Buddhism isn't quite so much fun as unruly Shintō, which peppers the calendar with carousing and partying during a plethora of annual festivals.

Whatever their differences, both Buddhist temples and Shintō shrines deal in *o-mamori*, designed specifically for warding off bad luck and evil spirits, and the trade is brisk. How odd. After all, religion to the modern Japanese is a matter of form and ceremony; it would be difficult to imagine a people who are more agnostic. Yet they are extremely superstitious. They consult fortune-tellers of all persuasions and often have *mamori* (you can optionally drop the honorific 'O' in English) dangling from the rear-view mirrors in cars and from key-chains and in their wallets.

Nearly everyone buys *mamori* in Japan; nobody believes but everyone wants to be on the safe side. Usually a small pouch made of brocade, the *mamori* is embroidered with the name of the shrine or temple. Inside it is a little wooden tablet and a paper prayer. They are sold in stores right inside the religious edifice or just outside it, arranged in boxes marked 'Traffic safety', 'Preservation from Sickness', 'Success in Exams', 'Prosperous business' and so on. The most expensive will be a combination. *O-mamori* sales are colossal just before students take their entrance exams for university. They buy them from the Shintō shrines around the nation called Tenmangu; these are dedicated to Sugawara-no-Michizane, a 10th-century scholar who died in wrongful exile and was subsequently deified as Tenjin, the patron of learning.

At New Year, Buddhist temples sell lucky wooden *daruma* dolls. Rotund and painted red and white (the colours of Shintō) they represent the legendary monk Bodhidharma, who brought Buddhism from India to China. One eye is blank—having made a wish, you fill in the other pupil if it comes true. Not strictly a *mamori*, the *daruma* is one of the talismans known as *engimono*. Sold at different times of year, they include those sold mainly at Shintō shrines. Among them the decorative *kumade* (a rake, for luck with raking in cash), the *hamaya* (a white arrow for driving evil spirits away throughout the

year), the *maneki-neko* (beckoning cat; see pages 122–123) and effigies of the Shichifukujin (the Seven Gods of Good Luck). Although also represented singly, the latter are in fact six gods and a goddess called Benten; mainly sold together aboard their treasure boat, they present quite a motley crew. Their origins are Shintōist, Buddhist, Chinese and Indian.

Engimono can be pretty strange. A popular item in the late 1990s was an effigy of the *bodhisattva* Jizō, guardian of travellers and the souls of children (see pages 118–119), presented as a bright-eyed cuddly toy made of grey plush. Out of all Japan's many thousands of Shintō shrines, some 40 odd are devoted still to phallicism and fertility. Made of candy, some of the *engimono* they sell there at festival time beggar description.

127

Koi Nobori

鯉幟

carp streamers

In spring, one of the most picturesque sights in Japan—especially in the country—are the gaily painted *koi nobori* (carp banners) seen floating over the rooftops. Decorations for Tango-no-Sekku, a boy's day festival that originated centuries ago and is held on the fifth day of the fifth month, the *koi nobori* are tied in tiers to long poles and set up to flutter in the breeze. The pole is decorated according to a set pattern: at the top is a streamer consisting of long coloured ribbons, beneath which is a black carp that symbolizes the father; just below it is a slightly smaller red carp symbolizing the first born son; next comes a carp for each successive son in descending order of size. *Koi nobori* dangle even from the balconies of high-rise apartment blocks.

Inside the house meanwhile, Tango-no-Sekku is celebrated with a display of *musha-ningyō* (warrior dolls). The male answer to the displays used for Hina Matsuri (Dolls' Festival or Girls' Day) on March 3rd (see pages 132–133), the dolls represent great samurai heroes of history and legend. Most prominent and combining both are Minamoto Yoshitsune (1159–89), the doomed hero of the Heike wars, often together with his loyal, gigantic sidekick, the warrior monk Benkei, a medieval samurai equivalent of the Incredible Hulk. The

dolls are accompanied by beautifully wrought miniature sets combining a samurai helmet with swords and armour.

The banners of Tangu-no-Sekku only later came to represent fish. Until the 18th century, they were based on the flags carried by samurai armies during battle campaigns. Once bearing little more than names and family crests, they gradually came to include paintings of heroes; indeed, on special occasions at Shintō shrines —for example, the festival in January when boys celebrate the *shichi-go-san* (7-5-3)—these hand-painted or stencilled *sashimono* (Boys' Day banners) are still made in modern Japan. With so many banners, Tango-no-Sekku is sometimes known as Flag Day.

Drawn up during the American Occupation in 1946, the new national constitution sought both to demilitarize and democratize a Japan poisoned by belligerence and chauvinism. The country was to renounce war for all time and women were granted the right to vote. It was deemed that celebrating maleness with displays of swords and armour was inappropriate; the product of a warrior culture, Tango-no-Sekku was accordingly given a much lower profile. Once exclusively for boys, the festivities of May 5th were incorporated in Children's Day (Kodomo-no-hi), a national holiday introduced

in 1948. Today families occasionally extend the *koi nobori* to embrace the female members of the household. Thus the big black carp is the father, the red one the mother and the others both boy and girl children. Whatever the concessions to sexual equality, however, it is telling that households with only female children never fly *koi nobori* at all.

If no longer intended to foster militaristic leanings, Tango-no-Sekku dominates behind the scenes of Children's Day. Girls still celebrate their own day on Hina Matsuri, so no one minds in the slightest. However, none would see the carp an appropriate symbol for a female. After all at Tagata Jinja, a famous phallic Shintō shrine near Nagoya, the image of carp swimming up a waterfall decorates votive plaques; the same design is what many *yakuza* gangsters choose for the tattoos adorning their backs. Like so many things Japanese, the symbolism of the carp harks back to China and an old legend. If a carp manages to swim up a waterfall, it will turn into a dragon. Thus the carp signifies strength and courage, perseverance and fortitude, all attributes once considered quintessentially male. The legend has no female dragons, thus the *koi nobori* is likely to remain a banner for manhood for the foreseeable future.

Origami

折り紙
origami

I recall a parting gift from the elderly landlady of a ramshackle *ryokan* on the West coast of Japan; she had made it herself, she said, it was her hobby. I marvelled at how she had fashioned a tiny doll representing a young woman in a kimono—using only one single sheet of multicoured paper. That I saw the same article in every store in town later that day was only slightly disappointing; the implication was that hers was a hobby shared by most of the town's female population.

Of all Japan's arts and crafts, probably the most popular is origami (paper-folding). Moreover, from the 1900s onwards, origami spread all over the world. Though there are exponents capable of making inspired and exquisite items both in and outside Japan, for the majority origami is rarely more than a casual pastime practised most commonly by schoolchildren. But not always. I once saw a drunk in a Tokyo bar make an origami doll out of a serviette and place it proudly on the counter; it was a figure with an outsize penis which moved up and down if you pinched its bottom. It's really amazing what can be done with a single sheet of paper! Any more, and it wouldn't really be origami. Every stationer's shop in Japan (see pages 74–77) sells packets of coloured and patterned paper specially for

origami; the real experts often paint and prepare the paper themselves—sometimes using sheets over 1 sq m (11 sq ft).

Until the 1880s, *ori* (fold) *gami* (paper) was known as *ori-kata*, the Way to Fold. It was a widespread hobby that had been practised for a very long time, almost as long as paper-making. So it comes as no surprise that origami originated in China. First invented by an imperial servant named Ts'ai Lun 2,000 years ago, paper came into Japan along with Buddhism during the mid 6th century. Not content with merely writing on it, the Chinese were already using the material for making boxes and various articles out of papier mâché, as well as exploring the possibilities of paper-folding. Having adopted all these things, it wasn't very long before the Japanese were adapting them.

Paper-folding found applications in both religious and secular contexts: the white zigzags of folded paper hanging from the *shimenawa* rope in Shintō shrines (see pages 112–113), the paper used in decorative charms at New Year and the carefully folded *noshi* paper used for wrapping ceremonial food (see pages 74–75). What became known as *ori-kata* soon became a pastime particularly popular with women. For many hundreds of

years the secrets of paper-folding had been handed down from mother to daughter until a manual, describing and illustrating the most popular designs, was published in 1797. Called *Hiden Senbazuru Orikata* or *The Secrets of Folding One Thousand Cranes)*, it is still in print 200 years later. By the time of the book's publication, the crane was the most common of many hundreds of designs suggesting other birds and animals, insects, human figures and assorted objects; today there are thousands.

Of all the origami figures, however, the most common is the most poignant: the *senbazuru* design, which represents a crane. *Sen* (thousand), *ba* (*wa* or *ba*—a grammatical counter for birds) and *zuru* (crane) refer to the bird which is a symbol of longevity in Japan. According to an old supersititon, when someone is ill, their condition will improve if you make 1,000 cranes for them. At Hiroshima, cranes in their hundreds of thousands festoon the memorial to those who died from the explosion and aftermath of the atomic bomb. Some of the survivors are still alive and still ailing; the *senbazuru* made by schoolchildren all over Japan are to wish for their recovery.

Hina Ningyō

雛人形
dressed dolls

Traditional western dolls, however finely crafted, mostly look like chubby babies; their Japanese counterparts usually look like adults —and those between 300- and 80-odd years old, most sought by collectors, are not even toys. They were produced by master crafts-people in workshops nationwide, in which there was often a specialist for the doll's faces and hands, another for hair and head-dresses, one more for textiles and clothes and another for accessories. Called *hina ningyō*, they were made for Hina Matsuri, the Doll Festival (Girls' Day) held on March 3rd—a custom that is still very much alive. Consequently, there are still workshops making them, notably in Kyoto and Tokyo; from hand-made masterpieces costing millions of yen to humble mass-produced dolls, they can be tailored to fit all budgets.

Relatives offer them to baby girls on their first Hina Matsuri and homes with female children display the dolls on special tiered shelves for most of April. Handed down from mother to daughter, *hina ningyō* (not to be confused with plain *ningyō* which means any kind of doll) are family heirlooms. Seated or standing and most properly aligned in entire sets, they sport exquisite finery, their faces delicately carved and whitened beneath carefully styled heads of real human hair. Collectively they

represent a court scene, with the O-dairibina, the prince and princess, sitting in state on the uppermost shelf. On the shelves beneath are their entourage—retainers and servants hold-ing swords and pikes, pouring sake or sitting around amidst minutely wrought articles of furniture in gold and black lacquer. Minuscule slivers of glass in their eyes complete a picture that seems uncannily realistic.

Dolls have a long history in Japan, as magical and ritual objects rather than toys. The rudimentary clay figurines of the Jōmon era (c. 10,000–300BC) were probably ritual objects; in the Yayoi period (300BC–300AD), the Japanese adopted the Chinese practice of placing figurines in tombs. Dolls continued to have magical connotations until only recently. Used in shamanistic exorcisms known as *oharai*, dolls called *hito gata* (human-shapes) were often placed by a child's bedside to ward off evil spirits. During Tango-no-Sekku, a male counterpart to Girls' Day (see pages 128–129) dolls representing warrior heroes are presented to boys, a custom thought to be rooted in the magical male 'guardian dolls' originating over 1,000 years ago.

The broader popularization of the custom of giving children fine *ningyō* is believed to have started during the early 15th century.

Enthroned when a year old on March 3rd, 1630, Meisho was the first empress for over 800 years. To mark the occasion, which was also Hina Matsuri, beautiful dolls were made for and presented to her by her uncle, the shogun Tokugawa Iemitsu (1604–1651). The samurai aristocracy followed suit and the custom spread like wild fire, so much so that during the 17th century sumptuary laws twice forbade commoners from the practice. The custom reached its apogee during the reign of the shogun Ienari (r. 1787–1837), who had over 50 children—most of them girls. After that, the sumptuary laws were wholly ignored. The *hina* dolls most prized by collectors were made during this period, though most of the items in antique shops today date from the Meiji era (1868–1912) or later.

Cha Dōgu

茶道具

tea ceremony utensils

Cha-no-yō or Sa-dō, the Way of Tea, is one of the greatest and most subtle of all Japanese arts. Or was. One might concede that a few genuine tea masters and teaists still remain, just as are there still potters and craftsmen making the tea-bowls and implements the tea ceremony commands. That said, the practice has largely degenerated. Filled with meanings long forgotten, it now pays slavish attention to the form but the content is lost. Time was when this was the preserve of high-ranking samurai, clerics and lofty literati; now an overwhelmingly feminine pursuit, the tea ceremony is in danger of becoming occupational therapy for frustrated housewives. Sa-dō gives them a reason to don a fine kimono and bask in a climate of elegant ritual of an afternoon; if you lived in one of those ubiquitous urban-industrial suburbs, the desire for such nostalgic excursions is readily understandable.

Okakura Kakuzō (1862–1913), a.k.a. Okakura Tenshin, predicted just such a state of affairs in 1906 in his famous Book of Tea, which remains one of the finest treatises on Japanese traditional culture written in the English language. A great arts scholar, Tenshin was a traditionalist who foresaw the impact the adoption of Western ways and means was about to have on oriental (and not just

Japanese) culture as a whole. Latterly Curator of Oriental Antiquities at the Boston Museum, Tenshin was, along with the American scholar Ernest Fenellosa, an important member of the group that founded the Tokyo School of Fine Arts in 1889. This was seen as a means to preserve Japan's threatened traditional arts. Esteemed for his brilliance and passion for his subject, Okakura was also an eccentric.

"One may be in the midst of the city," he wrote of the tea experience, "and yet feel as if he were in the forest far away from the dust and din of civilization." Critics have dismissed his vision of the tea ceremony as heavily idealized, but his basic concept was accurate. As a perfectionist, it was natural that he should only see it at its most esoteric and sophisticated. The influence that cha-no-yū had on Japanese aesthetics, Tenshin insisted, cannot be overestimated.

At the core of it all is Zen—a form of Mahayana Buddhism known in China as Ch'an and brought to Japan in the 13th century. Meanwhile, introduced by monks and popular among the Japanese clergy and aristocracy between the 8th and 11th centuries, tea drinking had fallen out of fashion. It was not to see a significant revival until the increase of commercial ties with China during the reign of

the shogun Ashikaga Yoshimitsu (1358–1408). The predilection for tea grew with a deepening interest in Zen; both were enthusiastically adopted by the ruling samurai caste.

Chinese monks used tea to stay awake during meditation; if it had become a ceremony at all, it was because anything done routinely and collectively in a monastery eventually becomes ritualized. Having adopted the concept, the Japanese typically improved upon it. By the end of the 15th century, the Way of Tea made quenching thirst a low priority. It had become an extraordinary aesthetic entertainment, an occasion where the arts and their various manifestations worked together in synergy. A form of art appreciation, it demanded a high level of erudition and sensitivity from its participants. Remote indeed from the staid, hollow ritual practised by those dutifully going through the motions today, it was also a kind of game. Fortunately, aspects such as the preparation and presentation of dishes specially for the ceremony still underlie Japan's finest culinary arts.

Sa-dō epitomizes the impact of Zen upon Japanese culture. The more creative followers found in the tea ceremony a forum in which their different talents and proclivities found relevance. Revering simplicity and naturalism, Zen prompted the idea that less is more. Cha-no-yū and its correlative arts always reflect wabi (quiet taste) and sabi (elegant simplicity). These are the criteria for shibui (sober refinement), the apogee of Japanese taste. Inspiring poets, calligraphers and painters, Zen helped elevate flower arrangement to the art form known as ikebana (see pages 38–39) and sent gardening into a realm approximating today's conceptual art. The epitome would be the famous rock garden of Ryoanji temple in Kyoto, which consists of nothing but a rectangular sea of raked gravel between four walls, with strategically placed rocks emerging from it like islands.

Rousing such cultural currents were the great tea masters, especially Sen-no-Rikyū (1522–1591), who established the canons for the ideal tea room. Spotless and plain, it should actually be a hut with an anteroom and tea room able to accommodate little more than five people, or four and a half tatami mats in size. There is typically a kakemono (hanging scroll) and a flower arrangement in the tokonoma alcove; often made to look plain and rough-finished to the point of almost belieing their craftsmanship, tea bowls (cha-wan) must be of the highest quality. All the elements should complement one another, but nothing should do anything so obvious as to match. No symmetry. If you use a round kettle, the water pitcher should be angular. A cup with a black glaze should not be associated with a tea caddy of black lacquer. If you have a flower arrangement, you cannot use a painting of flowers.

With a refreshing sour edge and a hint of bitterness, the subtly flavoured tea is called matcha. A powder, it is whisked to a bright green froth with hot water in a bowl. After a sip, the participant wipes the rim of the bowl and passes it on to his neighbour. As the iron kettle sang (they sometimes placed metal chips inside to make sure it did) atop a hibachi brazier (see pages 30–31), the party would guess at the provenance of the chinaware and the painting or calligraphy; there would be connections between these and the flower arrangement, the whole having to hint at and harmonize with the season and the weather.

Tea-houses had to have the proper surrounds, and this is where the gardening comes in. Teaist gardens balanced trees and plants, ponds and brooks and rocks and hillocks, as well as devising effects of light and shade. Reflecting Zen philosophy they conveyed the spontaneity of nature using elaborate artificial contrivances. Both a landscape gardener and architect, tea master Kobori Enshū (1579–1647) built the famous Katsura detached palace, now owned by the Imperial family and still standing today with its magnificent (but very simple) tea houses and gardens atop a hill outside Kyoto. It had been commissioned by the shogun Toyotomi Hideyoshi, who never lived to see it. Perhaps that is just as well; perhaps he wouldn't have liked it.

After all, when the tea master Sen-no-Rikyū fell from his favour, Hideyoshi forced him to commit suicide in 1591. The motive remains unknown, although one story has it that Hideyoshi's efforts to make a concubine of Rikyū's daughter were thwarted; another that Rikyū was falsely implicated in a plot to poison the shogun. One thing is certain however: what came between them first involved tea and taste. The shogun liked his tea ceremonies to reflect his wealth and power, which is to miss the point entirely. Having made the tyrant aware of the vulgarity of his aspirations, the tea master was doomed.

Kō and Kōro

香、香炉
incense and incense burners

Drawn with a Chinese character meaning 'fragrance', *kō* is the Japanese word for incense; *kōro* is the incense burner. Whether round or square, standing free or on a base, with shaped legs or without, the typical *kōro* is a small, low-sided ceramic jar. Made out of the same material or of metal, its lid is perforated to let the smoke through. If the lid is missing and the *kōro* is a valuable antique, it will occasionally be replaced with another made of wood. Representing subjects such as animals, birds and grotesques, during the late 19th century *kōro* were often made of bronze, specially designed for the Western market. Nowadays tasteless *kōro* (contrived as kewpie dolls, porcelain pink piggies, and so on) make their way even into the modern Japanese home. In those days the grossest taste was foreign and something artisans catered to extremely lucratively. Then, as now, a lot of Japanese would contend that an ornate or fanciful *kōro* is inappropriate in any case; its proper place is the *butsudan*—the Buddhist home altar (see page 116). For those who do not have a *kōro*, respects are paid at the *butsudan* simply by sticking joss-sticks into a pot of sand and ashes before it, and many leave incense burning anyhow and where they please simply because they like the fragrance.

Others don't like it at all. Like most things dealing with Buddhism, incense holds eerie, funereal connotations. This is epitomized by an old ghost story, about a despondent widower lighting incense to commemorate his recently deceased young wife. As a sinuous cloud streamed up from the burning incense and filled the room with fragrance, he perceived a shape materializing in the billowing vapour and gradually assuming human form. The image became clear; the spirit of his wife stood hovering in the smoke.

Be that as it may, the majority of Japanese have a predilection for incense—they have used it to perfume clothes and houses for centuries; cedarwood is popular as it is a moth-repellent. Incense is sold in supermarkets, the *butsudan-ya* (the shop specializing in Buddhist paraphernalia) or, if you can afford it, in the much rarer specialist shops.

Incense, you might think, is little more than smoke. In a country in which the fleeting cherry blossom is almost an object of worship, however, much is made of the ephemeral. So it isn't really so surprising that some Japanese revere incense as something approaching the sacred, and will spend small fortunes on rare varieties. One variety of *jin-kō* (aloes wood), for instance, is literally worth several times its weight in gold. Such enthusiasts are almost invariably practitioners of *kō-dō*—the Way of Incense—a rarefied olfactory equivalent to the tea ceremony. And as with the latter, the pursuit has become overwhelmingly feminine, the majority of practitioners being elderly.

A Japanese magazine recently put the current number of devotees at around 50,000; out of these a smaller (and doubtless wealthier) élite might belong to the two most important schools—the Shinoryū and its more exclusive parent, the Oieryū. Like schools of tea, *noh* or *ikebana* flower arrangement, incense schools are ruled by an *iemoto* (principal), a title that is bestowed almost exclusively on a hereditary basis. Hachiya Sōgen, the current head of the Shinoryū school, is the 20th generation. His ancestor was one Shino Munenobu, a friend and pupil of Sanjō Nishisanetaka, who launched the Oieryū; both schools were founded in Kyoto during the Muromachi era (1338–1573), when *kō-dō* became a pastime favoured by the ruling Ashikaga shoguns. Consisting of passing a *kōro* from one participant to another and trying to identify the incense, *kō-dō* is a game; it was by then already more than 500 years old. The sybaritic shogun Yoshimasa was particularly fond of *kō-dō* and was proud of being able to identify 135 different fragrances.

In the more ancient temples in the Kyoto-Nara, the glass cases in the treasure halls invariably exhibit chunks of wood so old they look in danger of falling to bits. Indeed, some of them are over 1,000 years old. They are rare and precious *kōboku*—incense woods famous for their fragrance throughout the ancient world. According to historical records commissioned by Shōtoku (574–622), prince regent to the empress Suiko, incense was first imported into Japan in the year 595.

By the early 8th century, incense was being used in secular contexts too; the Heian era (794–1185) was obsessed with it. Using it to perfume their rooms and clothes, they also turned its appreciation into something of a cult.

The period saw the blossoming of a sophisticated culture. It was a remarkable age, the Heian—as long as you were a member of the aristocracy. If you were, you were one of the very wealthy, beautifully attired and utterly languid *yoki-no-hito*—the good people; if you weren't, you hardly even existed. That would seem obvious from the volumes the *yoki-no-hito* wrote about their lives and times. The era's most significant writers were women: Sei Shōnagon's famous diary *The Pillow Book* made many insightful (and often extremely catty) remarks about life and people at court

and, published in AD 1000, Murasaki Shikibu's wonderful *Tale of Genji* transpired to be the world's oldest novel. The profligate hero, Prince Genji, was as fond of incense parties as any other courtier at the time. Murasaki outlined the preparations and practices such as leaving the *kōboku* buried in a jar for months (and even years) to improve its scent and blending the powders weeks beforehand, the recipes always being shrouded in secrecy. The contestants would carefully choose all the incense jars and boxes to make the most stylish presentation during the event.

The heroes and heroines competed keenly to produce the perfect scent. She writes: "Princess Asagao's was outstanding for its calm, elegant scent... the judge picked Genji's, which had an unusually full and nostalgic quality...." This detailed description of an incense party helped set the pattern for *kō-dō* adepts for all time. After some years of comparative neglect, it was this form of incense partying that became fashionable again in the 15th century in schools like the Oieryū and Shinoryū. It is no coincidence that the most popular of several incense-guessing games is the one called Genji-kō.

Involving five kinds of *kōboku* to be differently mixed in 25 packets, it seems

as complicated today as it always was. The master randomly picks five; the participants—permitted to take the *kōro* three times—must take up ink and brush to write the Chinese character (often just a meaningless symbol) corresponding to the mixture they think it is on a sheet of paper before them.

If you are interested in *kō-dō*, a word of warning. There is one thing you should never even contemplate. Incense is neither 'inhaled' nor 'sniffed'. Heaven forbid anything so uncouth as 'smelling' it. The proper verb is '*kiku*', which means to 'listen'. So when you play the game and they pass you the *kōro*, you write down the symbol for the incense you think you're hearing…

Bibliography

Akiyama, Terukazu, *La Peinture Japonaise: Les Trésors de l'Asie*, Editions Albert Skira, Genève, 1978

Bowers, Faubion, *Japanese Theatre*, Charles E.Tuttle Co., Vermont, Tokyo, 1974

Bornoff, Nicholas, *Pink Samurai – An Erotic Exploration of Japanese Society*, Grafton, HarperCollins, London, 1991; *National Geographic Traveler Series Guide to Japan*, National Geographic

Bushell, Raymond, *The Netsuke Handbook of Ueda Reikichi*, Charles E.Tuttle Co., Vermont, Tokyo, 1961

DeBecker, J.E., *The Nightless City – the History of the Yoshiwara Yûkwaku*, London, 1899 (Charles E.Tuttle Co., Vermont, Tokyo, 1971).

Dresser, Christopher, *Japan: Its Architecture, Art and Art Manufacture*, Longmans, Green & Co., London, 1882. (Reprinted as *Traditional Arts and Crafts of Japan*, Dover Publications Inc., New York, 1994)

Hibbett, Howard, *The Floating World in Japanese Fiction*, Oxford University Press, 1959 (Charles E.Tuttle Co., Vermont, Tokyo, 1975)

Kawabata, Yasunari, *The Master of Go*, Alfred A.Knopf, Inc., New York, 1972 (Charles E.Tuttle Co., Vermont, Tokyo, 1973)

Lane, Richard, *Images from the Floating World – the Japanese Print*, Office du Livre, Fribourg, Switzerland, 1978

Moes, Robert, *Mingei, Japanese Folk Art from the Brooklyn Museum Collection*, Universe Books, New York, 1985

Morris, Ivan, *The World of the Shining Prince – Court Life in Ancient Japan*, Alfred A.Knopf, Inc., New York, 1964 (Charles E.Tuttle Co., Vermont, Tokyo, 1978)

Morse, Edward, *Japan Day by Day Vol. I*, Houghton-Mifflin, 1915, 1945; *Japan Day by Day Vol. II*, Houghton-Mifflin, 1917, 1945 (*Vols I and II*, Cherokee Publishing Co., Atlanta, 1990); *Japanese Homes and their Surroundings*, Ticknor & Co., New York, 1886. (Dover Publications, Inc., New York, 1961)

Munsterberg, Hugo, *The Japanese Print*, John Weatherhill & Co., New York and Tokyo, 1982

Okakura, Kakuzo, *The Book of Tea*, Fox, Duffield & Co., New York, 1906 (Dover Publications Inc., New York, 1964)

Piggot, Juliet, *Japanese Mythology*, Hamlyn Publishing Group Ltd., London, 1969

Ponting, Herbert G., *In Lotus Land Japan*, MacMillan & Co., London, 1910.

Saito, Akio (editor), *A Look Into Japan*, Japan Travel Bureau, Inc., 1984; *Japan, the Official Guide*, Japan Travel Bureau Inc., 1952

Stevenson, John (with introduction by Donald Richie), *Yoshitoshi's Thirty-Six Ghosts*, Weatherhill, New York and Tokyo/Blue Tiger, Hong Kong, 1983

Tagai, Hideo, *Japanese Ceramics*, Hoikusha, Osaka, Japan 1976

Watson, William (editor), *The Great Japan Exhibition: Art of the Edo Period*, Royal Academy of Arts London, 1981–82

Watt, Andrew, *The Truth About Japan!*, Yen Books, Charles E.Tuttle Co., Vermont, Tokyo, 1988

Internet sources:
Maneki Neko, Alan Pate; L'Asie Exotique of La Jolla California, 1996. Antique Japanese Festival Dolls, T.Mertel; L'Asie Exotique, 1986. The Practice of Using Seals, William Lise; Japan Chopsticks and Wood, TED Studies.
Karuta, Sports or Culture? David Bull, 1996 (from Hyakunin Issho, internet newsletter by print artist David Bull). What is Hyotan? Article in Hyotan Newspaper, Hitachi, Japan. (Futon) Japan Trade Monthly Kimono Fujikawa web site.

Glossary

amado: wooden shutter

andon: box-shape lighting appliance

bakemono: ghosts/goblins (lit. 'changed things')

bentō: packed lunch box

bosatsu: bodhisattva

bunbōgu: stationery

butsudan: Buddhist home altar

butsudan-ya: shop selling Buddhist paraphernalia

byōbu: painted screen

cha-wan: tea bowl

chōchin: paper lantern

chōzubachi: stone water basin

dosojin: roadside deities

ema: votive plaque

engimono: talisman

furisode: kimono with long, baggy sleeves (for unmarried women)

furoshiki: cloth wrapping

fusuma: thick paper room divider; cupboard door

geta: wooden sandal

gokiburi: cockroach

hanakago: flower basket

hakimono: Japanese footwear

hanko: seal

hanten/happi: workman's jacket

hashi: chopsticks

hibachi: portable charcoal brazier

hina ningyō: dolls for Hina Matsuri

hyōtan: gourd

inkan: seal

inrō: medicine purse

ikebana: the art of flower arranging

irori: iron hearth

ishiku: stone mason

ishidōrō: stone lantern

kabuto: helmet (in armour)

kakemono: hanging scroll

kamidana: Shintō home shrine (lit. god-shelf)

karakuri: mechanical toys

kasa: umbrella

kanzashi: hair ornament

kō: incense

kōro: incense burner

koi nobori: carp banner

kura: storehouse

kushi: comb

mado: window; window cavity

maneki-neko: beckoning cat

menpō: iron mask (in armour)

miko: shrine maiden

minshuku: family-owned inn

mizuko: unborn foetus

mon: family crest

nabemono: pot stew

netsuke: toggle hanging from the obi

nihon-tō: Japanese curved sword

ningyō: doll

noh: masked drama

noren: entrance curtain

ōgi: folding fan

ojime: cord tightener

o-mamori: talisman to keep bearer safe from misfortune

origami: paper-folding

ro: small sunken fireplace

senbazuru: paper crane

setta: thong sandal made with woven rushes or tatami matting

shikki: lacquerware

shimenawa: sacred rope

shōji: latticed wood, sliding paper screen

suzuri-bako: writing box

taisha: grand shrine

tansu: wooden chest

tanuki: racoon-dog

tobi: fireman

tokonoma: alcove

tomesode: short-sleeved kimono (for married woman)

tsukubai: garden basin

tsuba: sword guard

tsuyu: rainy season

wagasa: Japanese umbrella, made of oiled paper over a bamboo frame

yakuza: gangster

yoroi: armour

yoshizu: marsh-reed screen

yukata: summer kimono

zazen: zen meditation

zōri: sandals worn with a kimono

Credits

With special thanks to:
Masami, for her encouragement and support; Monique Colahan; Leslie Downer; Michiko Rico Nosé; Mrs Kimura, Casa Kimura, Kokubunji; Madoka Shiraishi; Tawaraya Inn, Kyoto.

The Japanese Gallery
66D Kensington Church Street
London W8 4BY, UK
tel/fax: +44 20 7229 2934
23 Camden Passage, London N1 8EA
tel: +44 20 7226 3347

1-5-1, Fukushima-cho
Nishi-ku, Hiroshima City, Japan 733
tel: +81 82 231 6066

Katie Jones
195 Westbourne Grove,
London W11 2SB, UK
tel: +44 20 7243 5600
fax: +44 20 7243 4653
e-mail: kjoriental@lineone.net

Gregg Baker
132 Kensington Church Street,
London W8 4BH, UK
tel: +44 20 7221 3533
fax: +44 20 7221 4410
e-mail gbakerart@aol.com